# THE IRRATIONAL TERRORIST
### AND Other Persistent Terrorism Myths

# THE **IRRATIONAL TERRORIST**
## AND Other Persistent Terrorism Myths


Darren Hudson,
Arie Perliger, Riley Post,
and Zachary Hohman

LYNNE
RIENNER
PUBLISHERS

BOULDER
LONDON

Published in the United States of America in 2020 by
Lynne Rienner Publishers, Inc.
1800 30th Street, Boulder, Colorado 80301
www.rienner.com

and in the United Kingdom by
Lynne Rienner Publishers, Inc.
Gray's Inn House, 127 Clerkenwell Road, London EC1 5DB



**Library of Congress Cataloging-in-Publication Data**
Names: Hudson, Darren, 1970– author. | Perliger, Arie, author. | Post,
    Riley J., author. | Hohman, Zachary, 1982– author.
Title: The Irrational Terrorist : and Other Persistent Terrorism Myths /
    Darren Hudson, Arie Perliger, Riley Post, and Zachary Hohman.
Description: Boulder : Lynne Rienner Publishers, Inc., 2020. | Includes
    bibliographical references and index. |
Identifiers: LCCN 2019033915 | ISBN 9781626378490 (hardcover) | ISBN
    9781626378506 (paperback)
Subjects: LCSH: Terrorists. | Motivation (Psychology) | Human behavior.
Classification: LCC HV6431 .H844 2020 | DDC 363.32501/9—dc23
LC record available at https://lccn.loc.gov/2019033915

**British Cataloguing in Publication Data**
A Cataloguing in Publication record for this book
is available from the British Library.

Printed and bound in the United States of America

 The paper used in this publication meets the requirements
of the American National Standard for Permanence of
Paper for Printed Library Materials Z39.48-1992.

5  4  3  2  1

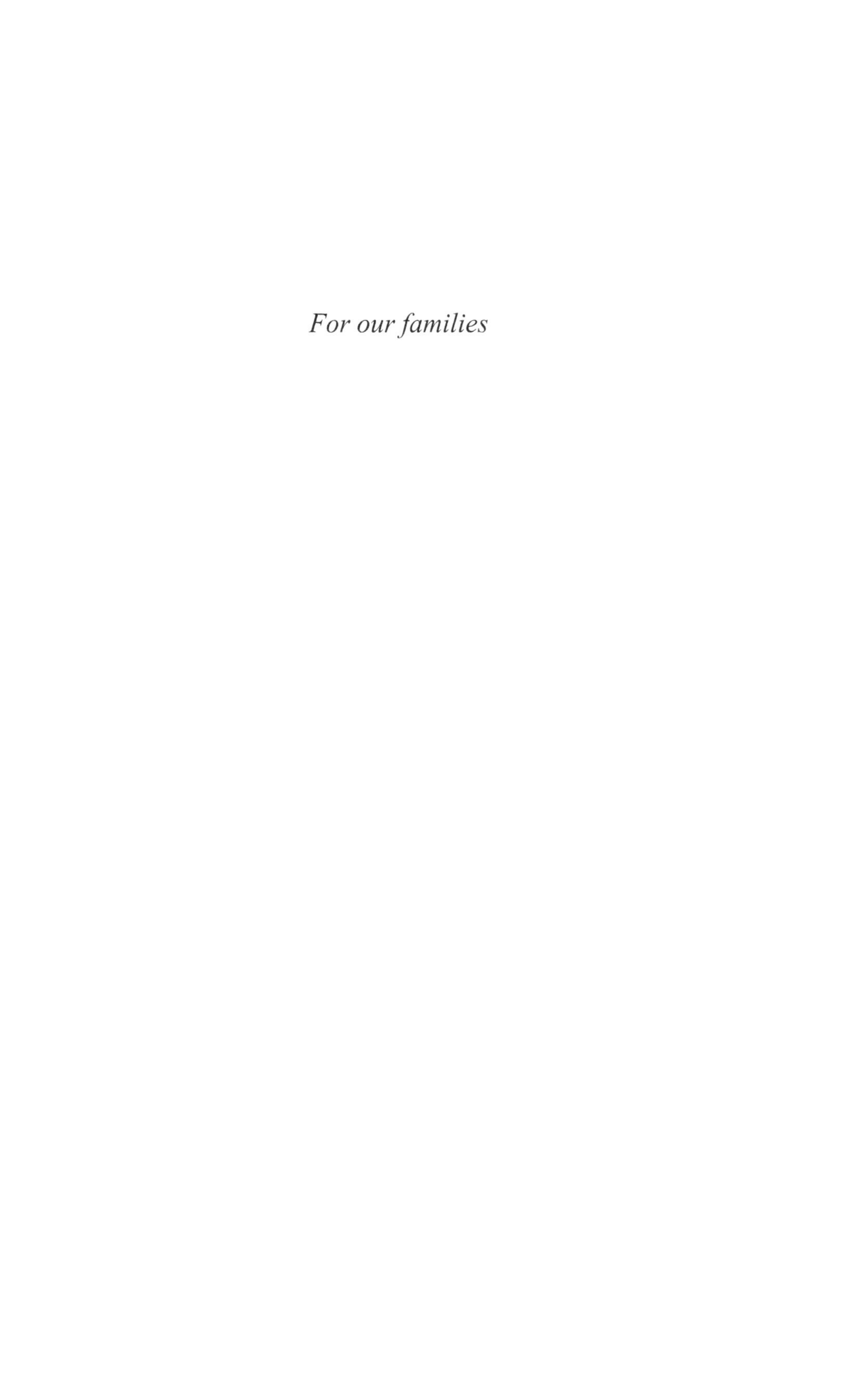

*For our families*

# Contents

# Tables and Figures

## Tables



## Figures

# 1

# What We Think We Know About Terrorism

The United States, and indeed the whole world, had its attention focused on terrorism in the wake of the September 11, 2001, attacks on the World Trade Center and the Pentagon. Terrorism likely only casually populated most minds prior to that date, despite the fact that as a social phenomenon it is as old as organized government. One of the most notorious and earliest organized terrorist groups was the Jewish Sicarii, which operated in Palestine against Roman occupiers in the first century AD. Others, such as the Assassins of Syria or the Thuggee of India, operated in the eleventh century. But the term *terrorism* is more modern and associated with the Reign of Terror that followed the 1789 French Revolution.

In relation to subjects such as chemistry, biology, or even economics, the field of terrorism studies is relatively young, beginning in earnest only in the 1960s with the rise of left-wing terrorist activities. Despite some important efforts by historians and political scientists, who mostly applied qualitative methods, at least some of the early efforts at understanding terrorism were riddled with erroneous assumptions and lack of data. Unfortunately, as in business and other realms of human endeavors, first movers usually set the tone of discussion, and those erroneous assumptions have perpetuated themselves in the form of persistent, pernicious myths. In terms of modern terrorism, for example, analysts and pundits initially suggested that the "religious wave" of terrorism in which we currently find ourselves somehow differs fundamentally from previous manifestations of terrorism because the motives behind the new terrorism appear religious and not political in nature. At the same time, terrorism appeared to spring from poor, uneducated areas of the world, leading to an assumption that economic/social grievances served as one root cause of terrorism by providing a wedge issue that religious groups were using to create a desire for social change. Both of these assumptions, as we shall discuss, are at best misleading and not supported by data.

As we discussed terrorism with friends and colleagues, we noticed that such misconceptions were generally coloring the public's views, which generally influenced what they saw as acceptable and appropriate responses. And because in most countries public perceptions and preferences impact public policy at some level, many of the myths about terrorism resulted in ineffective counterterrorism policies. For example, the belief that poverty undergirds modern terrorism has led to billions (perhaps trillions) of aid, development, and research funding aimed at poverty alleviation in a vain attempt to reduce terrorism. Thus, we felt it was time to address these myths head-on using the accumulated scientific literature as a backdrop, but in a way that any interested reader could easily access.

It is easy to understand why some of these myths persist through time. They fit our preconceptions or preferences. For example, imagining a logic or even rationality in the mass and/or indiscriminate murder of people can be incredibly difficult. If one watches or reads almost any public discourse on terrorism since 9/11, the term *crazy* is invariably invoked to suggest that terrorists are irrational people who blindly strike out against anyone in their path. After all, who in their right mind would murder for no apparent reason other than hate? But, as we will show in this book, that simply is not true. We are not asserting that terrorists are morally correct—far from it. Rather, we show that they do not fit the classical definitions of mental illness and instead exhibit rational behavior, given their objectives, both psychologically and economically.

Of course, all persistent generalizations contain grains of truth. But like many generalizations, these have taken on the status of myth with Jungian archetypes. That is, terrorism is cast in terms of "good" versus "evil" in a primal, innate way that prevents a deeper understanding of underlying causes. This analysis by no means excuses the choices made by terrorists or justifies their existence. Rather, breaking down root causes helps us target them for more effective counterterrorism that will give the "blood and treasure" devoted to it the highest effective return. We use modern psychology, economics, business, and political science to filter this mythology and see what stands up to scrutiny and what does not.

In this vein, we aim in writing this book to tackle some of the more persistent but pernicious myths about terrorism that are in fact impeding our development of adequate and successful counterterrorism policies. Our goal here is not to plow new theoretical ground but to fill the gap between the theoretical and empirical academic literature and the broader public literature in a way that is accessible. The writing is extensively sourced so that interested readers can further delve into the scientific literature as desired. Appendices and text boxes add a bit more context and analytical detail for those interested, but we hope that the writing itself provides a useful passage through the literature without being too burdened with jargon and the granular aspects of theoretical arguments.

Our journey begins, of course, with some basic background in Chapter 2. There is a misconception that we lack a comprehensive means to even define terrorism in the first place. Despite the debates in the scientific literature, we do at least have a consensus working definition that terrorism is "political violence." Definitions are important because they guide how political leaders respond when an event occurs, so we spend a bit of time addressing the base definitions. Some historical perspective also adds context to how and why we define terrorism.

The remaining chapters address some of the critical myths and issues related to terrorism. In Chapter 3 we tackle the elephant in the room that is always front and center in modern terrorism: religious fundamentalism. We talk about the role that religion plays—and does not play. Religion can serve as a fertile recruiting mechanism with its highly socialized structure and built-in motivations for behavior. But this sort of "cultural approach" to understanding terrorism ignores the most important aspect of the phenomenon: at its core, terrorism is a political activity. Understanding this distinction allows us to proceed to a better understanding of other critical misconceptions about terrorism. Because, at a base level, if we firmly believe that only religion causes people to act, dismissing other observable motivating factors becomes easy.

Chapter 4 examines the role of poverty and relative economic deprivation in terrorism. Despite the ease of envisioning the poor, hungry, and uneducated as highly motivated to change their circumstances and thus prime recruits for terrorism, the evidence just does not support this belief. And because it persists, we misdirect money and manpower. Chapter 5 addresses the impact of mental illness. Are terrorists irrational? Are they "crazy"? Again, we take on this myth directly. The belief that terrorists are irrational is comforting because then we can easily dismiss their behavior as anomalous. Unfortunately, the reality is not quite that simple.

Television punditry often greatly misrepresents the complexity of terrorist organizations, always positing one of two scenarios: complex interwoven cells spread across the world tightly coordinated by a terrorist leader from a cave in Afghanistan or rudimentary "lone wolf" actors blowing themselves up in crowded popular places. While both versions are partially accurate in some circumstances, these simplifications miss very important elements of organizational design and evolution that help us understand how we might better combat terrorist groups in the most effective ways. We address these issues in Chapter 6 by comparing terrorist groups and analyzing the role of networks and economics in organizational design. Chapter 7 focuses attention on the role of risk and media in shaping the public's view of terrorism. Here, we take on the very sensitive topic of how terrorists *and* governments can manipulate public response based on our innate reactions to and preferences for risk. We hope that an examination of how our personal preferences are used against us will make readers more discerning about information and arguments offered for actions and in managing their own reactions to terrorism itself.

A primary reason for tackling this subject is to better inform the public about terrorism and how that relates to effective counterterrorism policy. Chapter 8 therefore takes on some critical counterterrorism myths that are limiting the public's view of policy efficacy and the best path forward for addressing terrorism in the future. We wrap it all up in Chapter 9.

This book presumes neither that you know everything about terrorism nor that you know nothing. In some cases, we may uncomfortably challenge your preconceptions. We have no underlying agenda. Everything we discuss is fully supported (and documented) by the academic/scientific literature. We approach this issue dispassionately because we believe that having a clear-eyed view of what terrorism is and is not offers the best way to move forward in addressing it. And we do not claim that this is the end of the discussion. There is much to learn and much ongoing research. But at this juncture, we believe it is time to clear some of these myths from the common vernacular so that the understanding of terrorism and demands for counterterrorism policy stand more soundly on facts and not misconceptions.

# 2

# Myth: I Know Terrorism When I See It

One of the most enduring perceptions within the academic and policy communities, as well as among law enforcement practitioners, is that terrorism lacks a consensus definition. One of the best-known experts in the area of terrorism studies, Walter Laqueur, even advocated abandoning the quest for a consensus definition in favor of a better understanding of what terrorism is not, stating, "Years of debates on typologies and definitions have not enhanced our knowledge of the subject to a significant degree. If we cannot define terrorism, then we can at least usefully distinguish it from other types of violence and identify the characteristics that make terrorism the distinct phenomenon of political violence that it is."[1] Another way of describing the problem harkens back to a 1964 Supreme Court opinion in which Justice Potter Stewart remarked, "I shall not today attempt further to define the kinds of material I understand to be embraced within the shorthand description ['hard-core pornography'] and perhaps I could never succeed in intelligibly doing so. But I know it when I see it."[2]

A lack of definition is troublesome, however, because it means the term can morph, change, and be used in ways it was never intended, thereby making it extremely difficult to develop theories and frameworks for explaining its various aspects. For instance, in July 2013 the European Union (EU) designated the military wing of Hezbollah, a Shiite Lebanese organization, as a terrorist group. While Israel and the United States applauded the decision, both also expressed reservations about the EU's decision not to designate the entire organization as a terrorist entity. Benjamin Netanyahu, the Israeli prime minister, explained, "As far as the State of Israel is concerned, Hezbollah is one organization, the arms of which are indistinguishable." But multinational organizations such as the EU operate on compromise. While some states supported the designation of the entire organization as terrorist, others, such as Austria, Italy, and Ireland, were reluctant to make that call. The latter group of countries had peacekeeping forces in Lebanon and wanted to avoid exposing them to potential attacks by Hezbollah; they also felt that it was important to keep an open dialogue with the organization. The need for compromise in the European Union, the long time that passed before the decision was made (Hezbollah began engaging in violent operations in the early 1980s), and the contrast between EU perceptions and US and Israeli perceptions reveal the role of political symbolism and interests in most peoples' and states' conceptual framing of terrorism. But beyond these dynamics, the EU decision reflects the ongoing disagreements in the debate regarding the definition of terrorism itself.

Several reasons are usually presented to explain the inability of academics and practitioners to agree on a definition. These include the diverse ideological frameworks and tactics promoted and used by terrorist groups. For example, while in the 1970s many groups preferred to engage in aviation terrorism (hijacking) and hostage taking, mainly in the name of left-wing or nationalistic sentiments, recent decades have witnessed the rise of terrorist acts in the name of religious ideology. Many groups have abandoned hijacking and hostage taking in favor of more lethal tactics such as suicide operations.[3] The ideological-motivational diversity of the perpetrators of terrorism, combined with the ongoing change in how they operate, creates difficulties in clearly identifying the boundaries of the terrorism phenomenon.

Also clouding the effective definition of terrorism is the fact that rarely do the violent actions of groups that enjoy the support of national or international political institutions get designated as terrorism. For example, despite acts of violence against civilians perpetrated by the African National Congress (ANC) in order to promote its political objectives, countries outside South Africa never perceived it as a terrorist organization, and large constituencies admired its leaders, especially Nelson Mandela. Indeed, international condemnation of the apartheid regime facilitated the branding of the ANC as a civil rights rather than a terrorist organization.[4] Similarly, the support of Western countries and other international actors in the struggle against Bashar al-Assad's brutal regime in Syria probably was an important factor in the decision of Western political leaders and news media platforms to designate the anti-Assad groups as rebel or insurgency groups rather than terrorist groups. Indeed, we can understand why many identify with the phrase that President Ronald Reagan used in a speech at Camp David in May 1986: "One man's terrorist is another man's freedom fighter."

Lastly, the interdisciplinary nature and policy relevance of terrorism also seems to undermine attempts to provide conceptual clarity to this phenomenon. Because the field of terrorism studies incorporates different disciplinary backgrounds, different scholars have unsurprisingly framed the phenomenon in accordance with their own disciplinary analytical tools and thus focused on specific facets of terrorism. Hence, political scientists have traditionally focused on the impact of terrorism on political stability and processes, while communications scholars have explored groups' use of terrorism as a messaging mechanism to convey their demands and mobilize support. Moreover, the disciplinary dominance in the field seems to change over time. If in the past the proportion of historians and "soft" (employing qualitative methods) social scientists was substantial, today more "hard" (or quantitative, data-driven) social science seems to dominate terrorism studies. The close relationships between the community of terrorism scholars and the policy realm also did not help to promote the efforts to reach a consensus paradigm regarding the definition of terrorism. The tendency of government agencies to devise their own definitions of terrorism and related phenomena (see Chapter 7), as well as the inclination of academics to accept policy-driven definitions, led to a proliferation of different definitions, each reflecting the specific orientation of different government agencies.

While many continue to argue that our understanding of terrorism as a social phenomenon suffers from conceptual confusion and inconsistencies, and despite the disagreements between state actors regarding the designations of specific groups, we suggest that the perception that we lack consensus regarding the components that comprise the terrorism phenomenon is more myth than reality. Especially since 9/11, the myth is less and less grounded in the real world of academics and practitioners. This is not to say that we will not find works that fail to distinguish between insurgency and terrorism or between criminal organizations and terrorist networks, but for the most part today we can find a far-reaching consensus on at least the basic components of terrorism as psychological warfare involving violence against noncombatants with the aim of communicating a political message.

In the next sections of this chapter, we will discuss the historical evolution of the concept of terrorism, how we arrived at a working consensus, and what that means in terms of our understanding of the factors that impact the effectiveness of terrorism as a form of warfare.

## Terrorism in Historical Context

*Terrorism is a horrible thing and is the great threat to civilization on our planet.*

—Walter Isaacson

While some scholars argue that terrorism is likely as old as the human race, a closer examination reveals that before modern times, terrorism was mostly restricted to campaigns of political assassinations rather than the attention-grabbing attacks of our time. For example, the Sicarii, a Jewish fundamentalist cult, engaged in a campaign of assassinations against the Roman occupying force in Palestine in the middle of the first century AD, as well as against Jewish leaders who cooperated with the Roman administration. Similarly, the eleventh-century Assassins, a religious Islamic sect that originated in Shea Ismailism, were known mainly for their assassination campaign against Middle Eastern Sunni leaders hostile to Shia Islam. Roughly in the same historical period, the Thuggee, a secret cult that was active in India, engaged in an assassination campaign against travelers and other hostile ethnic/religious groups. The assassinations, in this case, manifested their worship of Kali (the goddess of destruction).[5]

But why did these historical groups gravitate toward assassinations and not other forms of violence? The answer seems to relate to some of the reasons that facilitated the fast proliferation and effectiveness of modern terrorism in the last 120 years.[6] Modern terrorists promote their political objectives by relying on an array of modern technologies to publicize their violent attacks, disseminate their ideology, and mobilize the masses. The lack of such technologies before the last couple of centuries basically required groups that wanted to directly influence a state's policies to bypass the psychological dimension of terrorism (i.e., use of violence to produce public pressure/support to convince policymakers to modify policies) by engaging in assassinations of political leaders. Assassinations can be effective in leading to policy changes without significant investment in garnering popular support or the creation of extensive recruitment mechanisms to exploit that support.[7]

Developments in military technology allow contemporary groups to cause significant harm to superior enemy forces or civilian targets. While groups such as the Sicarii or Assassins did not have such capabilities, engaging in assassinations allowed them to effectively promote political instability without the need to confront superior military forces or engage in sophisticated attacks against civilian infrastructure.

The concept of terrorism was absent from the political discourse probably until the French Revolution, when the modern concept of terrorism emerged to describe the exercise of fear and violence to promote political ideas. It is important to note that the Reign of Terror was a general term alluding to the brutal, arbitrary violence by the new revolutionary regime against opposition groups and figures.[8] It refers to another case of a new regime trying to consolidate its control over the general population and the political arena rather than the phenomenon that most of us today recognize as terrorism: violence to bring about political change.

The transition toward modern terrorism occurred in the mid- to late nineteenth century, when a group of scholars and public figures, led by individuals such as Carlo Pisacane, Mikhail Bakunin, and Sergey Nechaev, developed new frameworks of political philosophy that saw the exercise of violence as an important condition in any successful effort to change the political or social status quo. They argued that violence is not just a construct that must accompany any meaningful social change but a part of the process in which people internalize new political consciousness and acquire political capital, both of which are necessary components of every political or ideological revolution. Therefore, in their eyes, the violence serves both as an instrument to coerce enemies of the revolution and as "propaganda by deed," an instrument to spread the ideas of the revolution and instill them in the minds of the masses.[9]

While most leaders of the anarchist movement in the late nineteenth century opposed the use of violence and preferred mass protests and other forms of mass action, the influence of Bakunin and Nechaev, both influential thinkers within the movement, led some anarchist groups to conclude that "propaganda by deed" should also include direct violence. They aimed mainly to counter the actions of counterrevolutionaries in Europe during the late nineteenth century who tried to maintain the traditional ways of the monarch-based system. Similar to the Sicarii and Assassins, these groups also initially focused on tyrannicide, or the killing of the tyrant leader, but gradually acknowledged that "cutting off the head of the snake" was insufficient because most leaders can easily be replaced.[10] Therefore, these groups concluded there is also a need to direct the violence against the system that supports the tyrant.[11] Unsurprisingly, the anarchists' campaigns gradually expanded their target portfolios. For instance, Narodnaya Volya (peoples' will), probably the best-known violent anarchist group at that time, operated against the czarist regime in Russia. While best remembered for the assassination of Czar Alexander II, between 1879 and 1885 it also engaged in numerous acts of violence and vandalism against the symbols of czarist rule. These actions clearly reflected the anarchists' understanding that a broader, systematic campaign was necessary to effectively foment revolution.[12]

The anarchist violence was not particularly effective. While some anarchist groups were able to facilitate further instability within regimes that already suffered from a crisis of legitimacy (especially in czarist Russia), in no place were they able to mobilize a significant constituency. Eventually, they were overshadowed by nationalist and left-wing groups, which were more effective in communicating with the masses and mobilizing them against political elites. The "Anarchist Wave" of terrorism was followed by three additional waves, distinguished by the dominance of a specific ideological focus: anticolonial (1920s–1950s), new left (1950s–1970s), and religious (1970s–present).[13] An examination of these waves can provide important insights into the dynamics that facilitate the slide of some ideological movements into terrorism as well as the effectiveness of terrorism as a form of warfare.

Of all the previous waves over the last century, only the nationalist/anticolonial was generally successful. Most anticolonial violent struggles ended with the withdrawal of the colonizing state and the foundation of a new, independent polity. The National Liberation Front in Algeria was successful in leading to an independent Algerian state in 1964 after a seven-year struggle with France, and Jewish terrorist groups in Palestine, such as the Irgun and Stern Gang, engaged in violent campaigns that, among other factors, eventually forced the British to give up control of the country and led to the establishment of Israel. In contrast, the left-wing wave in the 1960s and 1970s had some sporadic achievements, mainly in third world countries, but even these were short-term as today communism has lost its relevancy in many ways and is not a viable competitor to the liberal democracies overwhelmingly predominant in the international system. While socialist movements are still influential, they rarely produce violent campaigns. Hence, today most left-wing terrorism manifests in the violence of some environmental groups. Lastly, it seems that jihadi terrorism, despite the intense and massive violence that it produced and its success in positioning itself as an acute security threat, can show very few long-term sustainable achievements, especially with the collapse of the Islamic State in Iraq and Syria (ISIS) in late 2017.

Why were the anticolonialists so successful? To begin with, most nationalist terrorist groups effectively exploited growing anticolonial sentiment both in the international community and among significant constituencies in colonial societies. In other words, with the end of World War II, colonies, which included massive populations that enjoyed limited political rights, became less and less legitimate and morally acceptable, thus less sustainable.[14] Moreover, because many perceived the violence of the anticolonial groups as legitimate, colonial powers found it difficult to justify the implementation of harsh counterterrorism measures. The success of the nationalist groups also related to the fact that they represented cohesive, identifiable constituencies that could be mobilized more easily because they were bonded by primordial/ethnic origins and identity. That means, unlike with the left-wing and jihadi groups, nationalist groups had to invest far fewer resources in convincing the people they represented that they deserved and should fight for basic collective rights such as self-determination. Lastly, most nationalist campaigns had, for the most part, clear objectives and an end-state goal. That political reforms could clearly end the violence provided a better framework for conciliatory processes and incentives for all parties, but mainly the colonial powers, to make concessions. In contrast, like the left-wing wave, the religious wave promotes the long-term revolutionary goal of completely altering the structure of today's politics and international system and thus provides less space for any conciliation processes. To paraphrase an oft-cited sentiment: "They are not interested in negotiation; they simply want to kill us."

Examination of the different waves also reveals that because terrorism is, at its core, psychological warfare that uses violence to communicate a political message, it is highly influenced by technological developments. The growing prominence of the online domain has allowed groups to operate on a global scale, in terms of both their operations and their recruitment efforts. Similarly, the growing reliance of modern infrastructure on computer networks has encouraged modern terrorist groups (and some state actors) to engage in what may be designated as "cyberterrorism." These developments, as well as changes in the strategic environment, have led many groups to modify their organizational structures. So, if in the 1960s most people perceived terrorist organizations as paramilitary groups with clear hierarchies and structures, today many experts acknowledge that independent home-grown radicals comprising a cell of a broader ideological movement are initiating many terrorist attacks.[15] These groups assume a flat or cellular structure with limited hierarchy and elusive boundaries (see Chapter 6). Lastly, it seems that if in the past groups mainly focused on operations that could maximize attention, many of today's groups seem to focus rather on maximizing the number of fatalities.[16] The proliferation in the last thirty-five years of tactics that include suicide operations and the use of human beings as "smart bombs" is a case in point. These changes have led many scholars to identify the fourth (religious) wave of terrorism as a "new" type of terrorism.[17] While there is still disagreement about how new the "new" terrorism really is,[18] in the last thirty years this wave has clearly influenced political and social dynamics all over the globe, and a growing number of countries see it as one of their most acute national security threats.

While 9/11 is the terrorist attack most associated with the fourth wave of terrorism, it is important to note that the phenomenon's origins relate to three major dynamics that gained momentum toward the end of the twentieth century. The first is the 1979 revolution in Iran, which eventually led to the consolidation of an Islamic republic, or theocracy, in the country. This event paved a path for other religious leaders in the Muslim world to foment theocratic revolutions, and the restoration of Islam to the center of the political arena became feasible. Moreover, the efforts of the Islamic Republic of Iran's leaders to export the revolution to new countries led eventually to the creation of new organizations all over the Middle East that are sponsored by Iran and committed to promoting its foreign policy.[19] The first example of this new strategy manifested as early as 1983, when Hezbollah, at the time still managed and directly supported by members of the Iranian Revolutionary Guards, used car bombs driven by suicide bombers to attack the US Marine and French military barracks in Beirut, Lebanon. The attacks resulted in a high number of fatalities (more than three hundred soldiers), which led to a withdrawal of the American-French peacekeeping force from Lebanon and to a major victory for Iran and the newly established organization.[20]

The second influential event was the end of the Cold War, which led to the creation of a new space for alternative ideological streams to rise, including Salafi-jihadism. Importantly, while the Muslim Brotherhood and the Islamist movement in general, as well as the Salafi-jihadi movement, were not born with the end of the Cold War, the decline of the Communist/Western democratic ideological division in the international system helped them find new relevance and expand their constituencies.[21] The early 1990s uncoincidentally saw the proliferation of jihadi militant thinkers and an increase in their influence, which eventually also led to actual attacks against Western targets, such as the 1993 World Trade Center car bombing and the 1996 Khobar Towers attack in Saudi Arabia. The drumbeat of a terrorist war was sounding. Finally, 2001 saw the largest terrorist attack in history. The 9/11 attacks changed the dynamics of counterterrorism globally. Until then, Western democracies had vacillated between acquiescence or even quiet support of terrorist activities and incoherent, uncoordinated responses. September 11, 2001, swiftly engendered the largest counterterrorism operation in history. Operation "Enduring Freedom" included the deployment of US-led coalition forces in Afghanistan in 2001 and 2002, which forced the collapse of the Taliban regime and eventually morphed into an ongoing low-intensity conflict with various organizations such as the Haqqani network and the Afghan Taliban.

The evolution of terrorism in the years since 9/11 illustrates the importance of the third process contributing to the emergence of the fourth wave. The impact of globalization in the social, economic, and political arenas in the last three decades led to a decline both in the role of the state in the political consciousness of the public and in the ability of states to maintain tight control over their populations' cultural, economic, and political attitudes. As state and nationalist sentiments lost ground, universal ideologies that aspired to mobilize transnational or international (e.g., religious or ethnic) communities and disregarded the traditional practices and borders of the international system filled the resulting vacuum. Hence, universal ideologies such as those promoted by jihadi-Salafists or militant environmentalists could more easily present their movements as viable alternatives to the existing national communities or identities and sought to supplant "the establishment" political systems.

Within the fourth wave, jihadi terrorism has captured the imagination of the Western world. Unlike the Shia-based terrorism of Hezbollah or the more regionally focused Sunni terrorism of Hamas, the Salafist school of thought seems to provide the most comprehensive infrastructure of violence. The growing attention also naturally led to the rise of new misconceptions regarding terrorism and specifically Islamic terrorism. As we will see later in this book, many of them are based on biased or incorrect perceptions of the jihadi threat and the rationale of terrorism.

## So What Is Terrorism?

The scenario tends to repeat itself every time another violent act generates a high number of casualties and gains national attention. Students, media, and the public ask, Is this terrorism? The Las Vegas shooting in October 2017, when Stephen Paddock shot at a crowd gathered for a country music event and killed 58 people while injuring more than 850, is one example. In another, immediately following the San Bernardino shooting in December 2015, a couple, seemingly inspired by ISIS propaganda, opened fire on the husband's colleagues gathered for a California Department of Public Health training event. They killed fourteen people and injured another twenty-two. Following such events the media calls experts for a quick "briefer" to provide background but are often looking for a quick quote to support their preconceived conclusions. Occasionally, politicians and policymakers also succumb to the temptation to include various acts of violence under the category of terrorism, despite their clearly limited familiarity with the discourse regarding the definition of the phenomenon.

Many believe that the lack of clarity regarding what terrorism is reflects the lack of clarity in the scholarly research on the subject. Indeed, since the late 1960s, when academics started exploring terrorism as a social phenomenon, numerous definitions emerged with no conclusive consensus.[22] The lack of a consensual definition was frequently used to justify the limited theoretical progress in the field, as well as the limited data gathered. Thus, the phrase "even academics and experts cannot agree on the definition of terrorism" became common and in many ways provided nonexperts the freedom to "play" with the concept and to apply it to various policy areas, such as narcotics (narco-terrorism), cyber (cyber-terrorism), and organized crime (criminal terrorism).

We argue, however, that the perception regarding the disagreement on the definition of terrorism, within both the academic and the policy communities, is overstated if not plainly inaccurate. It is one of the most enduring and damaging myths and misconceptions in the field of terrorism studies. A closer look at the discourse of the academic and policy literature on terrorism indicates there is more agreement than not about the main components of the phenomenon; any definitional disagreements simply reflect disagreements in definitions of broader social phenomena as well.

Most scholars of terrorism agree that at least four features are needed to characterize an event as a terrorist attack:

1. Includes the use of violence
2. Has political goals or context
3. Targets civilians and noncombatants
4. Aims to generate psychological impact[23]

Regardless of the specific tactic or strategy, the event must include some kind of physical or coercive violence (the latter refers to the threat of violence). While cases of direct physical violence constitute the majority of contemporary terrorist attacks, in the past that was not necessarily so. In the 1960 and 1970s, many terrorist groups assumed that hostage taking or hijacking planes could bring better attention to their grievances and struggle. The coercive violence, while not always generating direct physical harm to the hostages, manifests via the terrorists' forcing their will through the threat of direct physical violence and violating the basic freedoms of the hostages/victims.

A second component that characterizes terrorism is its political goals or context. These are not always easy to identify or draw conclusions about for two major reasons. First, it is not always clear what constitutes a political goal or how we should define what is political. Second, in some cases, the group's targets can include political figures or institutions, while its overall strategic and long-term objectives are not political in nature. Defining what is political is challenging. In many cases, confusion arises from failure to acknowledge that both traditional or formal politics and informal or noninstitutional politics are part of the same phenomenon. Politics, in essence, is the process by which collectives make decisions relevant to all their members, such as how to allocate goods, how to divide duties, and which services to provide.[24] Thus, politics exist in every setting in which a group makes collective decisions, be it in the family framework, the workplace, a social movement, or a nation. Terrorist violence is political in nature because it strives to change or preserve policies, norms, values, or practices that are relevant to a specific national, religious, or ethnic collective. Thus, whenever there are collective decisions there is politics—and where there is politics, there is the possibility of terrorism to influence politics.

At this point we can present at least three important conclusions. First, terrorist violence is not restricted to attacks against governmental targets or proxies. When on June 17, 2015, Dylann Roof killed nine worshipers at the Emanuel African Methodist Episcopal Church in downtown Charleston, South Carolina, he was motivated by a desire to change societal practices and laws guaranteeing equal rights to African Americans and to restore a legal system and political practices preferential to white Americans.[25] A political context clearly undergirded his violent act, making it a terrorist attack. Second, in contrast to some classifications in the literature on terrorism, religious fundamentalist groups are also political in their nature because they utilize their violence to promote specific practices and values within a specific religious community. ISIS, for example, desired to create a new political structure based on jihadi interpretations of Islamic religious texts and traditions that would replace the current secular nation-state framework within the Muslim world.

Third, it is crucial to differentiate between tactics that include some political dimensions and an overall strategy that is mainly criminal. For example, Mexican drug cartels most commonly target municipal mayors who dare to try to limit their freedom of action. For example, a short time after Juan Antonio Mayen Saucedo, the mayor of Jilotzingo (located around forty miles northwest of Mexico City), declared that he planned to act against illegal loggers who were devastating the municipality's forests, armed men affiliated with a local cartel assassinated him.[26] In such instances, the cartels attack political targets in pursuit of a criminal/financial objective. They target politicians who are threatening to undermine their ability to maximize their profits from criminal activities. They aim not to enhance their political power to influence policies but to ensure that they can continue increasing their profits from criminal enterprises. The cartels do not really represent any collective, just the material interests of their members. While their tactics have political context, their overall strategy and objective are not political; thus, their attacks are not terrorism but criminal violence.

The great majority of terrorism experts agree not just about the political nature of terrorist campaigns but also about the nature of their victims. Terrorism targets civilians and noncombatants, the latter being military personnel who are not in a battlefield environment, such as the victims of the November 5, 2009, shooting in Fort Hood, Texas, when Major Nidal Hasan, a military psychiatrist serving there, opened fire on fellow soldiers crowded in a Soldier Readiness Center. He killed thirteen and injured more than thirty. While the military initially looked at the event as workplace violence, the discovery that Hasan was exchanging communications with major operatives of al-Qaeda in the Arab Peninsula, such as Anwar al-Awlaki, and had expressed militant views prior to the attack eventually led to the recognition that the incident was indeed a terrorist attack.[27]

Finally, terrorist attacks aim to generate a psychological impact. Therefore, unlike with many conventional crimes, the victims are not of direct interest to the perpetrator, who is usually not familiar with them, and serve solely as an instrument to convey a political message to one or multiple audiences, such as policymakers, the perpetrator's community, or the general public. Hence, ISIS members who opened fire in the Bataclan Theatre in Paris on the evening of November 13, 2015, were not familiar with the people in the crowd; nor did they care whom they were trying to kill.[28] They simply viewed the eighty-nine fatalities and hundreds of injured as pawns in generating a psychological impact that more effectively spread the intended message. This lack of personal attachment explains why terrorists usually prefer to attack symbolic targets that can enhance the psychological impact of the attack and thus further influence the target audience. Symbolism is the reason why al-Qaeda chose symbols of the United States' economic strength and military might (the World Trade Center and the Pentagon, respectively) as its main targets in the 9/11 attacks.

Insurgency is generally based on the gradual formation of an alternative political structure by monopolizing control of specific peripheral territory (where the central government is weak). Insurgency groups hope to expand their state-like entity until they can directly challenge the regime they hope to replace. Terrorists differ from insurgency groups in their different operational practices, organizational structure, and interaction with the civilian population. Terrorists who aim to maximize the psychological impact of their attacks prefer to operate in dense urban areas, where they have access to symbolic targets and can ensure maximum exposure of their operations. Additionally, they prefer to operate as a civilian underground with no rank system or military structure because that is more beneficial for mingling/hiding within a civilian population (more on rational choice of structure in Chapter 6). In contrast, insurgencies mainly target military forces and law enforcement as well as assume a conventional military structure (part of their attempt to present themselves as a viable alternative to the existing regime) and operate in peripheral areas where they can engage in limited low-intensity attacks.

So, if there is agreement about the most fundamental features of terrorism, why do so many still assert that terrorism is a mostly ill-understood phenomenon? Because terrorism is a prominent policy issue that attracts many nonacademic experts from different areas, it is frequently a victim of misconceptions and conceptual overreach by people who may have policy experience but limited knowledge of the literature in the field (or are outright motivated to manipulate perceptions, as discussed in Chapter 7). In addition, the transformation of terrorism studies from a marginal niche into a heavily funded academic discipline attracted many new scholars to the field. Unfortunately, some of them invested limited effort in familiarizing themselves with past literature and the diverse facets of the phenomenon, which led to further inconsistencies in the literature especially in the decade after 9/11. Lastly, the difficulty conceptualizing terrorism is shared by many other social concepts, and as with most concepts in the social sciences, the closest we can get is an approximate definition. This, we contend, is exactly where we are with regard to the definition of terrorism.

## The Myth of State Terrorism

States are probably the most prolific producers of violence. After all, one characteristic of modern states is their monopoly on the legitimate and lawful use of violence in their territories. In most democracies, the government will utilize its proxies (i.e., law enforcement agencies) to exercise violent practices aiming to curb criminal activities, enforce the law, and maintain public safety. However, in authoritarian regimes, the violence is used not just to combat deviance from the law but in a systematic manner to ensure the survival of the regime and to undermine any potential for political opposition. Thus, violence aims to terrorize the public and opposition parties and to ensure conformity with the ruling ideology.

But can violence by the state be defined as terrorism? Some scholars answer in the positive.[29] After all, what many describe as state terrorism includes all major components of terrorism, such as a political objective, psychological impact, and the tendency to focus on civilian targets. However, the answer is not that simple. A main justification for clear conceptualization of a social phenomenon is that this allows us to develop effective theories to explain it. In other words, if we can put under the same category multiple manifestations of the phenomenon, it is easier to identify its explanatory factors and to develop related theories. Yet state terrorism cannot be explained with the same theoretical frameworks that help identify the root causes of terrorism. The set of calculations that lead a substate organization to use violence against the state and the public in most cases differs fundamentally from the set of calculations and dynamics that explain formal political leaders' decision to resort to violence against citizens. In addition, many of the limitations and constraints that lead weak and marginalized communities to try to advance their objectives in a violent manner do not really exist in the state's decisionmaking process about whether or not to use systematic forms of violence.

Several examples can illustrate these arguments. During the Syrian civil war, the Assad regime utilized violence against civilian communities in order to force their loyalty to the regime, even when jihadist and rebel groups contested its rule. Much of the mass killing of civilians, however, also aimed at eliminating ethnic and religious communities suspected of challenging the regime, such as the Kurd population. In other words, for the Assad regime, direct violence against civilian communities was clearly justifiable as they represented a continued threat and disloyalty. By contrast, the Kurds and other rebel groups based their decision to initiate a violent campaign against Assad on demands for recognition of the ongoing marginalization of large segments of the Syrian population, the impact of economic instability, especially in rural areas shortly before the outbreak of the war, and the support that these groups managed to mobilize from external actors. Thus, while the Syrian regime definitely employed violence to terrorize enemy constituencies, the rationale for the violence was not that of substate terrorism. Similarly, we cannot use the same theoretical framework to explain Joseph Stalin's regime of terror, when dozens of millions of Soviet citizens were subjected to punishments for their supposed lack of loyalty to the Communist Party, and the emergence in the 1990s of Chechen terrorism against Russia. The social and political factors are fundamentally different, despite the fact that in both cases civilians were terrorized.

## Metric of Terrorism's Effectiveness and Related Misconceptions

Between 1998 and 2001 al-Qaeda conducted a string of successful attacks against highly strategic and symbolic American targets. Starting with the simultaneous attacks against the American embassies in Dar es Salaam and Nairobi, continuing with the attack on the USS *Cole* in the port of Aden in 2000, and culminating with the 9/11 attacks, the organization killed more than 3,000 people and demonstrated its capacity to harm the military, diplomatic, and financial assets of the United States. Nonetheless, by early 2003 almost the entire military infrastructure of the organization was in ruins and its leadership on the run. These dynamics indicate that when engaging in terrorism, unlike with many other types of warfare, success on the tactical level rarely translates to strategic achievements. Simply put, while many terrorist organizations are highly successful in producing violent campaigns, most fail to achieve sustainable political gains.

The United States' success in destroying most of al-Qaeda's military infrastructure is not the only way to assess the effectiveness of its "War on Terror." While unable to maintain its material and military assets, al-Qaeda was able to further popularize the jihadi ideology. Al-Qaeda attacks between 1998 and 2001 dramatically enhanced awareness of and familiarity with the jihadi narrative and inspired the creation of multiple successful affiliates that eventually continued the struggle and expanded the geographical reach of the jihadi movement. So, while in 2001 America's enemy was one organization based in a specific territory, today the United States faces the challenge of countering the efforts of more than two dozen jihadi organizations all over the globe, most pursing primarily local goals but presenting global challenges to antiterrorism actors with limited resources.

---

**Figure 2.1    Approximate Number of Terrorist Incidents Annually Around the Globe, 1970–2017**

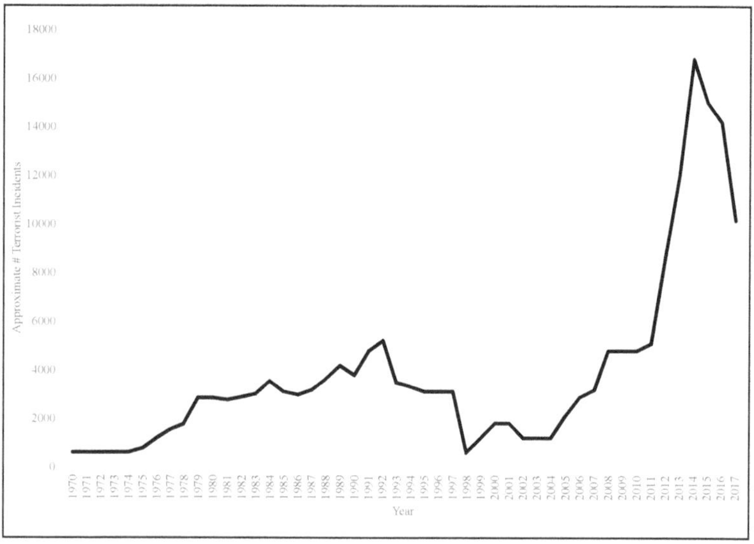

*Source:* Authors, data acquired from Global Terrorism Database, University of Maryland.

Terrorist incidents have grown over time, as Figure 2.1 shows, and especially since around 2004. Much of the post-2004 growth occurred in the Middle East region and targeted pro-US governments in Iraq and Afghanistan (and multinational security and law enforcement forces). But even if we break out those regions, there was an observable increase in other areas around the globe over the same period. This ancillary increase may be tied to the wars in

*continued*

Iraq and Afghanistan, but not directly. Whatever the root cause, the observed increase is important because it shows the dramatic increase in activity and the scope of the counterterrorism activities required to address the rise. (See also the appendix to this chapter.)

Was al-Qaeda's campaign effective? Or is the success of terrorism a myth? Should we examine how quickly the United States was able to destroy al-Qaeda's military camps and prevent attacks on the homeland? Or should we look at how quickly al-Qaeda was able to develop new affiliates and further popularize the jihadi narrative leading to the growth of total terrorist activities? These questions illustrate the complexity of evaluating the effectiveness of terrorist campaigns. Moreover, beyond the gaps between tactical success and strategic/political victory, the difficulty in assessing the effectiveness of terrorism also relates to the larger challenge of identifying causality between violent campaigns and social and political processes. For example, in 2000 Israel decided to withdraw from southern Lebanon after more than fifteen years of military struggle with Hezbollah. While some may attribute this decision to the cumulative effect of Hezbollah's attacks on Israeli military forces and civilians in southern Lebanon and northern Israel, most Israeli researchers argue that changes within Israeli society, which led to the strengthening of antiwar social movements, eventually led to Israel's withdrawal from Lebanon and to its decision to redeploy the Israeli military across the international border. The causality between the two events (or sets of events) is almost impossible to discern. We have witnessed a decline in terrorist activities in recent years. Does this decline relate to US drawdowns in Iraq and Afghanistan or to other reasons?

Can a completely different set of issues help us gain an understanding of the effectiveness of terrorism? For example, because terrorist organizations are political entities that aspire to promote the objectives of a specific community or collective, it may be important also to look at how a violent campaign impacted the level of support for the group and its leadership or maybe overall support for the ideological agenda of the group. Others prefer to assess more strictly operational aspects to evaluate the effectiveness of terrorist groups, including their durability and ability to produce violence consistently.

So how can we develop better and more nuanced tools to understand the effectiveness of terrorist campaigns? One possibility is to differentiate between two concepts related to the overall effectiveness of a terrorist group. The first is productivity, which reflects the organization's ability to produce attacks that generate significant psychological impact and to develop resiliency, both of which, in turn, ensure its durability. The second concept is political effectiveness, which relates to the group's ability to make progress toward the implementation of its political agenda. These two concepts are not necessarily correlated. For example, while the Palestinian Liberation Organization (PLO) was highly productive of terrorist attacks from the late 1960s to the early 1980s, it was not politically effective as it made no meaningful progress toward Palestinian political independence. In the early 1990s, following growing unrest and mass violence in the West Bank and Gaza, Israel eventually relented and started to negotiate with the PLO, a process that led to the foundation of the Palestinian National Authority (PNA). While the PNA is not a sovereign state, its foundation still represented an important step forward for the PLO, as it was recognized as the sole representative of the Palestinian people and Israel recognized the Palestinians' collective political rights. Thus, in the 1990s, the PLO was politically effective although not overly productive.

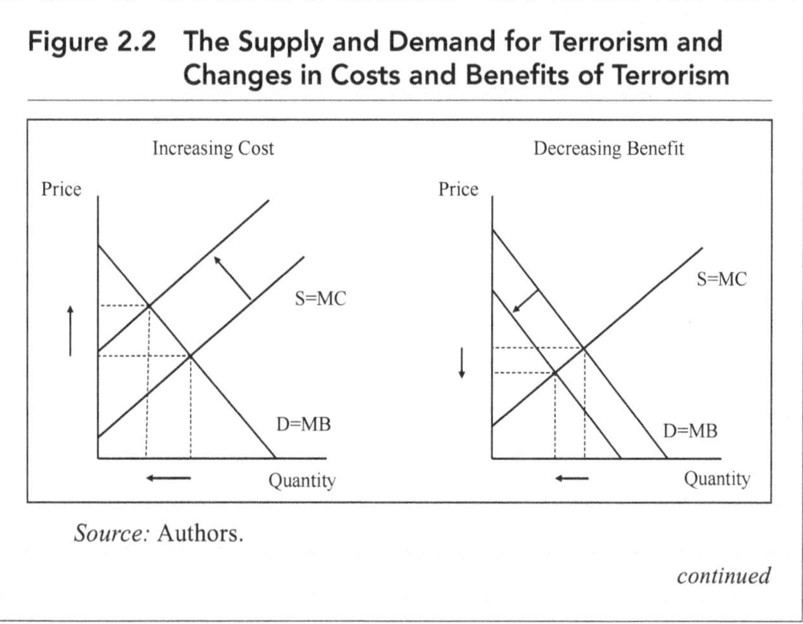

**Figure 2.2    The Supply and Demand for Terrorism and Changes in Costs and Benefits of Terrorism**



*Source:* Authors.

*continued*

> Believe it or not, terrorists "supply" terrorism in much the same way a firm supplies cereal or cars. There is a "cost of production," or the marginal cost (MC) in the figure. "Price" in this context is not the standard idea of price in a market but rather represents what benefits terrorists get from supplying terrorism. As these benefits rise, more people are willing to supply terrorism. Likewise, there are "demanders" of terrorism. These people want or receive benefits from terrorist activities. Betterment of life or social position, changes in relative deprivation or access to resources, changes to political power positions, and so forth, are all potential benefits. As the "price" they have to pay for these benefits increases, they will "demand less," or vice versa (see Figure 2.2). Clearly, if we can increase the marginal cost of supplying terrorism, we should see less of it. Conversely, if we can lower the benefits of terrorism, we can decrease terrorism as well. Policy has largely focused on the former rather than the latter.

Economics also can enhance our understanding of terrorism at both the individual and the group levels. There is a cost of "producing" terrorism, and as the "price" (think benefits to the group) rise, we expect to see more terrorist activity. But as costs of operating rise, we expect to see less activity. Counterterrorism efforts have focused heavily on increasing these costs, be it through military activities that have scattered leadership and training activities or killed key leaders or through security measures such as enhanced airport screening or increased law enforcement activities. The purpose is clearly to increase the cost of operations in hopes of reducing the supply and decreasing terrorist activities.

Nonetheless, we often forget there is a "marginal benefit" or demand for terrorism.[30] Why do people support terrorism (either financially or with their lives) in the first place? What benefits could accrue from such activity? Here, our public discourse has wandered very far afield and often led us to misunderstand the demand side of this equation. Religion, poverty, insanity, and so forth have all been proffered as explanations for why people would demand such activities. These, however, are but myths, as the following chapters will discuss. And because the public continues to believe in these myths, policy has woefully missed the mark in attempting to "lower the benefits" of terrorism, thereby decreasing the demand for the activity in the first place.

## Concluding Remarks

In the following sections of the book, we analyze various misconceptions and myths related to the contemporary discourse on terrorism and counterterrorism. In this context, we also emphasize that while terrorism is an important security threat, two important characteristics of the phenomenon must be recognized. The first is that terrorist organizations do not survive for a long time. While we are all familiar with organizations that have been active for multiple decades, such as al-Qaeda, Hezbollah, and Fuerzas Armadas Revolucionarias de Colombia, these are outliers that gained fame exactly because they have been with us for long periods. Yet, as social scientists have demonstrated repeatedly, most groups find it difficult to survive more than several years. Second, it is important to acknowledge that terrorism is not, in most instances, an existential threat to nation-states, at least directly. Rarely are terrorist groups able to replace state leaders or to transform a political system, and for the most part, state actors have been able to prevent terrorist campaigns from escalating into a threat to the regime. Remembering these two simple facts will allow us to look into the nature of terrorism with a sober and pragmatic mind-set. Lastly, it is important to admit that many of the misconceptions that will be discussed are also a by-product of political views and attitudes. In other words, much as our political views impact the way we frame and understand political and social issues, as well as their necessary solutions, in the case of understanding terrorism, bias resulting from political inclination is common and, in many cases, influences what we see as appropriate solutions. Thus, in this book we intentionally refrain from discussing politically motivated views and perceptions of the phenomenon of terrorism.

## Appendix to Chapter 2

Figure 2.2 describes a basic supply/demand formulation for terrorism. A more technical description is warranted for those most interested in the more nuanced theoretical relationships. Any supply function represents the marginal cost (MC) of production of a good (in the short run). So in a normal profit function, $\pi = PY - rX$, $P$ is the output price, $Y$ is the production function, and $r$ is the cost of input $X$. We will delve more deeply into the terrorist production function in Chapter 6. Suffice it to say here that the amount of terrorism produced is a function of both the benefits ($PY$) and the costs ($rX$). As discussed in this chapter, counterterrorism is largely aimed at increasing the cost ($rX$) of terrorism.

On the other side, demand reflects the marginal benefit (MB). This is likely a bit harder to visualize for most. How can terrorism generate a benefit? Agents of change can benefit from the instability resulting from terrorism. Chaos can generate public demands for concession to promote peace. Successful terrorism can improve recruitment and promote signals to broader groups and constituencies (Chapter 7). The key here is not to overly constrain one's thinking about benefits so as to enable more creative understanding of how groups potentially benefit.

Of course, in the end, the market of terrorism moves toward an equilibrium where the marginal benefits are equal to the marginal costs. If MB > MC, then terrorists are leaving benefits unexploited or ungained and will seek to increase terrorism produced. If MC > MB, the costs outweigh the benefits, and terrorists will be forced to reduce production.

Obviously, we want to reduce terrorism (although it is unlikely and probably uneconomic to completely eliminate it, as discussed in Chapter 9). But we can accomplish this by either raising the costs of production or lowering the benefits (or both). Shifting MC to the right (increasing costs) requires activities such that costs of production rise (e.g., enhanced security, higher risk of death or capture, etc.). Shifting the MB to the left (lowering benefits) requires activities such that benefits of terrorism are decreased (e.g., enhanced quality of life, improved opportunities for people, more inclusive government, etc.). Much of the rest of this book discusses these activities.

## Notes

1. Schmid and Longman 2005.
2. *Jacobellis v. Ohio*, 378 U.S. at 197 (Steward, J., concurring).
3. Of course, 9/11 was an aviation operation, but it was a suicide operation as well as a hijacking with hostage taking.
4. Boehmer 2005.
5. Hoffman 2006; Rapoport 1983.
6. Crenshaw 1981.
7. Perliger 2017.
8. Rapoport 2013.
9. Garrison 2004.
10. We might infer that their leadership was fairly weak if their enemies viewed them as largely expendable. For more, see Jensen 2013.
11. von Borcke 1982.
12. Davis 1962.
13. Rapoport 2013.

14. The astute reader is probably questioning causality here: Did anticolonial terrorism lead to the fall of colonialism? Or did declining support for colonialism give license to anticolonial terrorism to speed the process along? We offer no conclusion here, just the observation that anticolonial terrorism is the only wave with legitimate claims to widespread success.

15. Sageman 2004; Koschade 2006; Raufer 2003.

16. Laqeur 1999.

17. Kurz 2003.

18. Duyvesteyn 2004.

19. Panah 2007.

20. Marine Corps Association n.d.

21. Wiktorowicz 2006.

22. Weinberg, Pedahzur, and Hirsch-Hoefler 2004.

23. Hoffman 2006; Weinberg, Pedahzur, and Hirsch-Hoefler 2004; Schmid and Longman 2005.

24. Hague and Harrop 2013.

25. Perez-Peña 2017.

26. Reina 2016.

27. Readers should note here as well that the public and the media want immediate designations of events. But by gathering evidence and controlling emotions, we can arrive at more conclusive decisions about events and motivations and prevent incorrect or even harmful responses. Ghaneabassiri 2010; Jenkins 2010.

28. Bogacheva 2016.

29. George 1991; Selden and So 2004.

30. Readers are cautioned here not to mix the supply/demand for terrorism with the supply/demand for terrorists. The former is a market for political violence, while the latter is a labor market, which is clearly derived from the market for violence. We will cover both markets in the book.

# 3

# Myth: Religious Fundamentalism Is the Only Source of Terrorism

In late September 1982, a multinational military force (USMNF) composed of American, French, and Italian troops deployed to Lebanon. The escalation of the Lebanese civil war between a coalition of Muslim-Palestinian forces and Christian militias, as well as the growing involvement of foreign actors in the conflict (mainly Israeli and Syrian forces), had led to the decision of the international community to deploy the USMNF.[1] Formally, its mission was to help the Lebanese government and military regain control of the country and also to facilitate the withdrawal of foreign military forces from Lebanon. Informally, the Americans and French also hoped to use their presence to counter the growing influence of Iran and other Shia militant actors in the country and to prevent the Soviets from exploiting the war to expand their footprint in the region.[2]

## The Myth

While the deploying forces understood that they were arriving in a hostile environment, none of the commanding officers could predict that they faced the emergence of a new kind of threat: fundamentalist, religious terrorism, perpetrated through high-profile attacks against symbols of Western power and influence. Until the arrival of the USMNF, conventional insurgency attacks and targeted assassinations had mainly characterized the civil war.[3] That changed on April 18, when a suicide bomber drove a van loaded with 2,000 pounds of explosives into the lobby of the American embassy in Beirut. As a result of the explosion, large parts of the horseshoe-shaped building collapsed, exposing the interior and killing sixty-three people (several of them CIA officers working in the agency's local station).[4]

Despite the obvious threat in the unique operational environment, the USMNF fell victim to an almost identical attack only months later. On the morning of October 23, 1983, a large truck loaded with more than 12,000 pounds of TNT crashed through the perimeter of the USMNF compound at Beirut International Airport, broke into the 8th Marines Battalion Headquarters building, and was detonated by its driver. A few minutes later, French forces only two miles away suffered a similar attack against their barracks. As a result of the attacks, the buildings on both sites collapsed, killing 241 American soldiers and 58 French paratroopers.[5] A Defense Department review concluded that preparations were inadequate for the risks present; this sort of hindsight review only serves to reinforce the point that commanders were generally unaware of the new strategic risks posed by this new form of terrorism.[6]

In the following years, growing evidence indicated that a Shia militia, supported by Iran, was responsible for the attacks. This militia would eventually become known as Hezbollah—one of the most durable and capable terrorist organizations the world has ever known. Since the early 1980s, Hezbollah has managed to gain political representation within the Lebanese political system and to develop impressive military capabilities, as demonstrated by its ongoing military confrontations with Israel and, since 2011, against rebel and jihadi forces in Syria.[7] Nevertheless, the attacks in Lebanon had a broader meaning—they symbolized the outbreak of a new form of substate violence that most academics termed the "new terrorism." The concept of new terrorism reflected the growing prominence of religious fundamentalist groups, which are more inclined to operate globally and disregard international legal norms and practices (i.e., national sovereignty), adopt a cellular structure, and embrace especially lethal tactics that maximize the casualties of their attacks.[8] Unfortunately, however, the "religious wave" of terrorism also facilitated some significant misconceptions. In particular, many assumed that because this wave was religiously based, it was fundamentally different—that it was not political. As a part of this perception, people began to believe in the notion of "global jihad," or that this wave of terrorism was a global, not a local, phenomenon. Finally, the very nature of the "religious wave" was believed to emanate from religion itself. After all, Osama bin Laden often talked about the global jihad and the religious imperatives of martyrdom and self-sacrifice. These made for an almost nihilist view of terrorism.

## An Overview of Islam

It is sometimes easy to get lost in the names associated with Islam and terrorist groups. It is often useful to have just a brief synopsis to keep the names straight. There are two broad families under the umbrella of Islam—*Sunni* and *Shia* (using common English spellings). One might think of these as different denominations of the Christian faith, each sharing considerable overlap in doctrine, but with important differences in emphasis on things such as saints and prophets versus the written religious texts. But, in Islam, the major split occurred much earlier and the differences have become more distinct over time. And, like other religions, each "branch of the family tree" has a heterogeneous makeup, from relatively progressive to very fundamentalist.

Under the *Sunni* branch, there are more extreme versions, most related to *Wahabbism*, which has given rise to more radical and extreme interpretations of Islam from groups such as the *Salafists*. Terrorism within the *Sunni* branch ranges from the largely political (*Hamas*) to the very extreme creation of a caliphate through annihilation of other states (*ISIS*). *Shia* terrorism also has ranges of extremity, but the most famous *Shia* group, *Hezbollah*, has operated in largely political terms for considerable time, although it maintains an active military wing conducting operations against Israel as well as, most recently, *ISIS*.

*Sunni* members represent about 80% of Muslims worldwide, and naturally make up the lion's share of terrorist groups as well. *al-Qaeda*, *Al Shabab*, *Boko Haram*, *ISIS*, etc., are all *Sunni* (or *Salafist*) terrorist groups. The global scale of *Sunni* Islam offers recruiting grounds for potential terrorists on a far-reaching basis. But, as discussed here, the association of terrorism with a particular sect (or members of a sect) may be a matter of convenience rather than specific ideology.

## Upon Further Examination

With the growing prominence of terrorist groups aspiring to represent religious communities, more and more scholars and practitioners started to distinguish between political or secular terrorism and religious terrorism, insisting on the need for this division because religious groups tend to ignore national borders and operate globally.[9] However, a closer look at contemporary religious terrorist groups and their campaigns shows that the assertions about religious/political divisions lack empirical support. In reality, most prominent religious terrorist groups do not engage in global campaigns and pursue domestic political aspirations. The distinctions between political and religious terrorism simply reflect misconception rather than observed reality.

Let's begin by clarifying what differentiates religious from secular terrorism. Religious groups are unique in the sense that religious and sacred texts are at the center of all group activities. That is, religious groups legitimize and rationalize their use of violence with their own interpretation of religious texts. The religious practices and norms enhance the solidarity between the group's members and help to solidify the commitment of the members to the group's goals (a topic we return to in Chapter 5). Lastly, religious texts are also employed to draw the boundaries of the constituency the group strives to represent.[10]

But using a holy text does not make a group nonpolitical. To begin with, these groups represent a collective and operate in order to advance its interests (in their eyes), like most political actors. Most religious terrorist groups provide, via their actions and propaganda, a broad ideology that encompasses various aspects of the collective's social, political, and economic activities. Like a political party, violent religious groups package their views and preferences regarding various issues, including how to allocate public goods, how to structure the government, the major threats to the collective, the appropriate response to these threats, and their preferences regarding morality and ethics, specifically for their audience. For example, the Hamas charter provides a broad overview of the future Palestinian state and emphasizes Islam's relevance to all facets of the future Palestinian society. Article 2 states, "It [Hamas] is characterized by its deep understanding, accurate comprehension and its complete embrace of all Islamic concepts of all aspects of life, culture, creed, politics, economics, education, society, justice and judgment, the spreading of Islam, education, art, information, science of the occult and conversion to Islam."[11]

The Algerian Armed Islamic Group (GIA), the most brutal antigovernment group during the Algerian civil war in the 1990s, similarly sought not to promote specific religious concepts but to transform the Algerian state. This is why GIA never participated in the various peace initiatives promoted during the war and adamantly advocated for a full transformation of Algeria's society and political system. The leader of the group made this clear in a statement in December 1992: "We reject the religion of democracy. We affirm that political pluralism is equal to sedition. It has never been our intention to participate in elections or enter parliament. Besides, the right to legislate belongs solely to God."[12]

If politics refers to the process by which collective decisions are made and the related struggles for power and influence, then in most countries religious groups are entrenched in it. Organizations such as Hezbollah, Hamas, and the Muslim Brotherhood have participated in electoral processes and, in general, competed with other organizations for the privilege of making decisions for the collective they strive to represent. The idea that religious terrorist groups are not political is a pernicious myth that clouds a better, less emotional understanding of modern terrorism. Religious terrorist groups do not fundamentally differ from other violent political actors. They simply rationalize their violence with convictions and interpretations of religious texts. Once we understand that, we can move beyond the emotional entanglements of religious dogmatic differences toward an understanding of the political aims of these groups.

## The "Global Jihad" That Wasn't

If we can agree that religious terrorist groups are as political as secular terrorist entities, we can also partially understand why, despite their potential global outreach—Hezbollah, for example, can potentially strive to represent Shiites from different parts of the Muslim world—many of them still embrace national sentiments and frame their objectives in domestic and national terms. The first religious terrorist group to merge nationalist and religious sentiments was Hezbollah, which since the early 1980s has shaped an ideological agenda combining strong religious fundamentalist concepts, Lebanese nationalism, and commitment to the promotion of the interests of the Shia community in Lebanon.[13] While originally established to bring the ideas of the Iranian Islamic revolution to Lebanon, the organization quickly transformed

**Figure 3.1  Venn Diagram of the Intersection of Politics, Religion, and Violence**

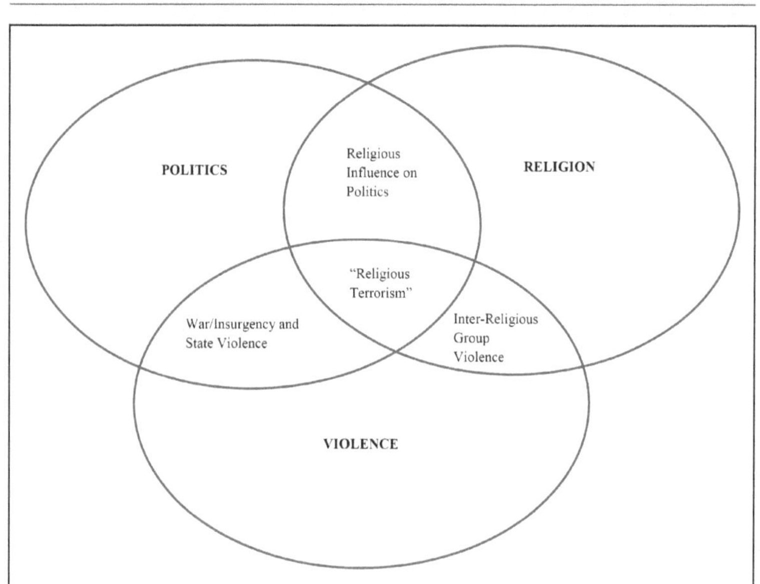


*Source:* Authors.

Although simplistic by design, Figure 3.1 illustrates the implications of the intersection of the variables we are discussing: politics, religion, and violence. Politics and violence often interact, resulting in all-out war or state violence as well as smaller conflicts, such as insurgencies or civil conflict. Religion and violence often interact to generate religious violence such as conflict between different religious groups or sects. Politics and religion can mix, giving rise to state-sponsored religions (such as in England or Israel) and even full-blown theocracies.

But the unique combination of religion interacting with (attempting to act through) politics through the use of violence manifests itself as "religious terrorism." Terrorism certainly need not be based in religion, as we have seen, but this is a useful way to think about how religion interacts with other variables to generate what we observe and think of as religious-based terrorism.

itself into one that fought fiercely for the territorial integrity of Lebanon and the country's strategic interests, especially against what adherents defined as Israeli occupation and threats. Additional elements that assisted Hezbollah in solidifying its Lebanese identity were its participation in electoral processes (which led to representation in parliament and the executive branch) and its sponsorship of a wide array of social services[14] for the Lebanese population in the southern and eastern parts of the country.[15]

Other known religious terrorist organizations followed the path of Hezbollah. Hamas, initially established as the Palestinian chapter of the Muslim Brotherhood, combined in its ideology a commitment to the realization of Palestinian self-determination via the creation of an independent Palestinian state, while also manifesting full commitment to the notion that any polity in the Muslim world, including a Palestinian state, should be run in accordance with sharia law and Islamic traditions and practices.[16] Once the Palestinian National Authority (PNA) was established, Hamas also became an actor in the formal Palestinian political system and in 2006 actually won the elections for the legislative branch of the PNA (the organization won 74 seats out of the 132 in the Palestinian Legislative Council).[17] Today, Hamas presents itself as the religious wing of a national liberation movement. Thus, the two most durable (and arguably capable and influential) religious terrorist groups in the Middle East, which are also among the few that were able to translate their violent capabilities into political representation and control over territory, actually emphasized and invested in their commitment to the interests of a national collective rather than some kind of a global struggle. This is not to say that they will not cooperate with foreign actors and movements or engage in direct assistance to strategic allies (as is the case with many nationalist organizations), but their reason for existence and most of their infrastructure are directed at promoting domestic and national interests.

The jihadi movement in general represents a complex reality. Indeed, many commentators tend to emphasize the global dimension of jihadism and its delegitimization of the concept of the nation-state. Moreover, some jihadi organizations clearly aim specifically to establish a global network for their violence and recruitment operations.[18] However, it is important to remember that ISIS and al-Qaeda do not encompass the entire jihadi landscape, and even within their networks, it is possible to identify the strong domestic and national nature of some of their affiliated groups. While Boko Haram pledged allegiance to ISIS in 2015, it continued to focus on its domestic campaigns against the Nigerian regime and its desire to found an Islamic state in Nigeria. The organization thus strives to transform the political landscape in the country to undermine the economic and social dominance of the Christian south and to impose strict Islamic cultural and social norms throughout Nigeria. Regardless of the organization's ties to other jihadi groups and its members' perceived acknowledgment that it is a part of a global jihadi struggle, it is still fundamentally a local organization that aims to promote local political and social objectives.

Many of the various affiliates of ISIS and al-Qaeda in the Maghreb have similarly never really operated outside North Africa and collaborate with local tribes and political factions rather than aspiring to serve their sponsor organization's global campaign.[19] This dynamic is not much different from the one that characterized Afghanistan in the early 1980s, when dominant warlords embraced the jihadi and Islamist narratives to gain access to Saudi and Pakistani funding and support; however, none ever had any aspiration to operate outside the Afghan arena and mainly focused on their tribe/ethnic group's (or personal) interests within Afghan politics.[20] Afghan leaders such as Gulbuddin Hekmatyar, Burhanuddin Rabbani, and Jalaluddin Haqqani are cases in point. All embraced jihadi norms and practices and emphasized their devotion to Islamist Afghanistan in order to facilitate and maintain the immense logistical and financial support that they received from the Saudi intelligence apparatus and Pakistani ISI or intelligence service (which in the 1980s became increasingly populated by Islamist commanders). However, they never aspired to be or saw themselves as anything but Afghan patriots.[21]

The domestic nature of religious terrorism is also apparent in prominent non-Islamic religious terrorist groups active in the last several decades. The Christian Identity movement in the United States, the most militant religious group in the country, is a prime example. An extension of the British-Israelite movement that emerged in the United Kingdom in the mid-nineteenth century, it advocates nativism, anti-Semitism, and white supremacy through distinctive interpretations of religious texts.[22] The various groups that comprise the movement utilize spurious religious heritage, symbols, ritual, and norms to popularize their beliefs and ideology.

However, despite the fact that the movement's ideological narrative and rhetoric discuss the "white race" at large and identify rival outgroups based on racial and ethnic characteristics and not national ones, much of its rhetoric, activities, and violent campaigns focus on race relations in the United States and, more specifically, on restoring what it deems the appropriate racial hierarchy in the United States.[23] Ironically, unlike its counterparts within the American white supremacy sphere, such as the skinheads and neo-Nazis, which developed extensive relationships with non-American white supremacy groups and even established branches outside the United States, Christian Identity never aspired to expand beyond the domestic American arena.[24]

Our last example of the strong presence of nationalistic components within religious violent groups is the case of Jewish religious terrorism in Israel. From the 1980s, multiple militant groups of Jewish settlers engaged in violence against the Palestinian population in the West Bank. The members of these groups belonged to a strain of Orthodox Jews who adopted messianic beliefs and regarded the realization of the vision of the Greater Land of Israel by means of Jewish settlement in the West Bank as a decisive phase in the salvation of the People of Israel and the foundation of a Jewish Kingdom.[25] More specifically, they believed that the tremendous Israeli military victory in the 1967 war was part of an ongoing holy redemption process, which began with the emergence of the Zionist movement in the late nineteenth century and its unpredictable success and continued to manifest with the success of the Israeli state to overcome substantial threats, including during its war of independence.[26] The Israeli military triumph of 1967, which restored Jewish control of important Jewish religious sites, especially the Temple Mount (where, according to Jewish tradition, the first and the second biblical Jewish temples were standing), was perceived as another step in the redemption process that many believed could be expedited by settling Jews all over the land of Israel and rebuilding the Jewish Temple in Jerusalem.[27]

These beliefs led members of this sect to engage in violent resistance when Israeli governments were willing to make territorial concessions to Arab countries or the Palestinians. In their eyes, because any territorial concessions in the land of Israel contradict God's commitment to the Jewish people as manifested in the ongoing redemption process, as well as an array of religious observations and commandments, they should be resisted and are not legitimate.[28] Between the 1980s and 2000s, several of these groups perpetrated campaigns of violence against Palestinian leaders and the population in order to disrupt the reconciliation processes between Israel and the Palestinians. Some of their attacks were highly sophisticated, such as simultaneous assassination attempts against Palestinian mayors in the West Bank in June 1980 by a group known as the Jewish Underground and a series of road attacks in the early 2000s by a group known as the Bat-Ayin Underground.[29] All these groups shared a common rhetoric and goals focused specifically on ensuring the realization of their vision of the future state of Israel; none was operating in the name of global Jewish goals. They embraced a nationalistic agenda rationalized via religious texts and traditions.

The global jihad, then, is largely a mythical notion. To be sure, religion of all stripes is often used as a catalyst for action, and there are sometimes appeals to struggles or goals larger than the immediate group or nation. But, as the late US House of Representatives Speaker Tip O'Neal once said, "All politics is local." So, to understand the development of terrorist groups, even religious ones, we need to understand the local area politics.

## Religion Is Usually a Cover for Political Motivations

The growing prominence of religious terrorist groups worldwide and their perceived ability to destabilize existing regimes led to an influx of scholars engaged in investigating and exploring the root causes of religious terrorism. They developed macro theories that hypothesized fundamental cultural and primordial characteristics of religion, and especially Islam, as a major driver of violence. This cultural approach relied on classical texts (such as Samuel Huntington's *The Clash of Civilizations*[30]) in order to illuminate the almost unavoidable violence arising from the continuing interactions between collectives from different cultural backgrounds and practices. Evidence seems to show that schisms between distinctive religious communities correlate with the intensity of violence.[31] Scholars also assert that political elites use religion to galvanize their followers. Its effectiveness as a mobilization tool relies on imagery related to the purity and divinity of sacred practices and norms.[32] Lastly, some scholars have analyzed religious texts to illustrate their inherently exclusive and populist nature, which facilitate hostility toward out-groups.[33]

The cultural approach only gained limited support among academics. However, a significant proportion of policymakers and practitioners quickly embraced it, feeling that a "clash of civilizations" perspective provided an effective way to explain the new landscape of global and domestic terrorism.[34] The civilizational struggle makes it possible for governments (and terrorists) to tap into the inherent perceived threat/anxiety dichotomy and to shape responses (see Chapter 7). Shortly after 9/11, various decisionmakers described the attack as a direct assault on the liberal-democratic world and its values by a foreign culture led by militant movements.[35] The rise of Islamophobic incidents in many Western countries in the years following 9/11 reflects the internalization of these views by a portion of Western societies. This civilizational dynamic also led to increasing support for far-right parties, which gladly embraced 9/11 and subsequent attacks as proof that the West is in the midst of a zero-sum game/clash of civilizations with the Muslim world.[36]

Many analysts of political violence were more skeptical about the cultural explanations and gradually collected data that contradict the view that religious violence is motivated exclusively by religious sentiments and norms.[37] More specifically, they presented evidence of peaceful coexistence among different religious communities for centuries in many parts of the world as well as of the prominence of intrareligious violence in many conflicts.[38] Most notably, most violence perpetrated by Muslims targets other Muslims. As scholars gathered more information on the structure and dynamics of the new religious militant movements, they demonstrated that outbreaks of religious violence often lacked the top-down planning necessary for an instrumental use of religion.[39]

The momentum against the viability of the cultural explanation has increased in recent years as scholars identified the political factors that underlie many religious conflicts. They found that globalization, modernization, economic disparity, territorial occupation, and communal suffrage mediate between religion and the outbreak of violence.[40] Ultimately, poor governance allows these catalysts to increase violence/conflict.[41] On the communal level, an association emerged between religious violence and in-group cohesiveness in religious communities, threat perceptions,[42] and animosity toward out-groups.[43]

Evidence, then, rejects the cultural approach and emphasizes the political nature of religious violence. The phenomenon of suicide terrorism, for example, was for many years considered a result of religious fanaticism and indoctrination. After all, only people completely convinced by and committed to narratives of the afterlife and religious martyrdom would willingly sacrifice their lives for a collective cause. But actual empirical data about organizations that use suicide attacks make clear that such beliefs do not tell the entire story of suicide bombing. For example, the majority of suicide-bombing campaigns have occurred in the context of (real or perceived) long and oppressive foreign occupation.[44] Groups affiliated with Kurds in southern Turkey, Palestinians in the occupied territories, Tamils in northeast Sri Lanka, and Chechens during the Chechnya war used suicide attacks as part of a campaign to end what they perceived as a foreign occupation.[45]

Similar dynamics can explain suicide attacks in Iraq until the American withdrawal in 2011. Most of the "occupying" countries in Iraq were democracies (with different levels of commitment to liberal practices). The vulnerability of democratic regimes to effective campaigns of violence and their difficulty in bridging liberal values and legitimizing their control of foreign territories contribute to a potential rationale for the use of suicide attacks in Iraq.[46] An organizational logic and political context, and not just pure religious devotion, facilitate campaigns of suicide attacks.[47] The fact that many of the "producers" of suicide attacks are actually secular organizations, which are not led by religious figures, further reinforces this conclusion. Among the most prominent are the Palestinian Fatah, the Kurdistan Workers' Party, and the Liberation Tigers of Tamil Eelam.[48]

The American Far Right provides an additional example of how religion serves an instrumental purpose but is not a motivating factor in terrorist activity. While all white supremacy groups in the United States support and promote policies to maintain what they perceive as the superiority of white people and object to any initiatives to advance diversity and inclusiveness in the social, political, and economic spheres, they use different sources of authority to justify their views. Neo-Nazis base their views on the pseudoscientific National Socialist ideology, while skinheads focus more on the economic marginalization of the white middle class.[49] In contrast, Christian Identity groups use unique interpretations of religious texts to justify their anti-Semitic and racist sentiments, as well as their hostility toward LGBTQ communities and liberal secularism in general. In the Christian Identity case, elites manipulate(d) religion to ensure the privileges of specific in-group members. However, in-depth study of the American Far Right reveals strong cooperation, coordination, and membership overlap between Christian Identity groups and other secular white supremacy groups.[50] This overlap reflects the limited role of a religious motivation in the political activism of members of these groups and the religious instrumentalization of their leaders. To illustrate, while the Aryan Nations was initially established as an Identity group, across time, its ideology transformed into a combination of neo-Nazi and Identity ideas. Indeed, most of its members seem to lack any particular religious affinity.

The upshot here is that there is more than meets the eye in the relationship between terrorism and religion. Some actors find it alluring, convenient, and even useful to blame religion and a clash of civilizations for the modern manifestation of terrorism. But the data do not support this oversimplification. This is not to say that the individuals involved in terrorism derive no inspiration or motivation from religion; rather, there is little evidence that religion alone gives rise to terrorism.

## Why Do Westerners Join the Jihad?

If religion per se cannot explain most outbreaks of conflict between religious collectives, can it be a factor in individuals' radicalization and joining of religious militant groups and movements? Examination of empirical findings seems to shed doubts on this as well. Individuals who leave their homes in Western democracies to join local jihadi groups in other parts of the world comprise a useful potential study group.

The crown jewel of the jihadists' success in terms of recruitment and mobilization is their ability to convince thousands of young Muslims from all over the globe to travel to the Middle East and join their ranks. Their success is especially impressive in that many of these young Muslims reside in developed Western countries and decide to travel to the Middle East to fight under harsh conditions while risking their lives for the jihadi cause.[51] The need to solve the puzzle of the jihadists' foreign fighters became more urgent in 2014 and 2015, when some of them returned to their home countries and perpetrated terrorist attacks.

Probably the first foreign fighter to return to his home country and perpetrate an attack was Mehdi Nemmouch, who in May 2014 shot to death four civilians at the entrance to the Jewish Museum of Belgium in Brussels. French authorities arrested Nemmouch six days later and eventually gathered enough evidence to definitively connect him to the attack. The follow-up investigation revealed that he had traveled to the Middle East and served in ISIS's ranks, where he helped guard Western hostages (who called him "Abu Omar the Hitter" because of his tendency to torture them as well as to brag about his involvement in ISIS's past operations, which included the raping of women and killing of babies). Eventually, ISIS leaders concluded that he was too unreliable and "let him go."[52] The specific motivation for his return to Europe is unknown, but his actions reflect his interest in utilizing the operational experience he gained while fighting in Syria. Similar events in the following months further elevated the concern of Western law enforcement, exemplified strongly by the words of the head of Britain's Office for Security and Counterterrorism, Charles Farr, who asserted that foreign fighter returnees are the "biggest challenge to UK security services since 9/11."[53]

Some scholars and practitioners emphasized the role of identity and ideology in foreign fighters' decision to join jihadi groups. One conclusion maintained that Saudi foreign fighters "are the product of a pan-Islamic identity movement that grew strong in the 1970s Arab world from elite competition among exiled Islamists in international

Islamic organizations and Muslim regimes."[54] The belief held that they join jihadi groups in order to express their commitment to an imagined transnational community whose boundaries are shaped by jihadi ideologies. Additional studies provided similar explanations; for example, one study found similar dynamics among foreign fighters from the Balkans.[55] But it is important to note that these studies looked at foreign fighters from Muslim countries, which are, on average, more educated and more affluent than their Western counterparts. Indeed, a somewhat different picture emerges from analysis of the background of Western foreign fighters.

One fact leading to skepticism about the role of religion as a motivational factor is that most Western foreign fighters have limited familiarity with Islamic theology and the jihadi narrative more specifically.[56] The great majority of the Western Muslim foreign fighters only began observing religious practices and norms a few months before their departure for the Middle East, and only a small portion of them had any formal religious education.[57] Thus, in many ways they were no different from other young adults in their communities, and many adopted a completely Western lifestyle before embracing radical views. This does not mean that identity does not play a factor in their radicalization process, but their capacity to develop an emotional and perceptual connection with the jihadi cause stems from their cultural and political circumstances as Muslims in Western societies rather than on religious ones (we will return to some of these concepts in Chapter 5). It is not surprising then that much of the narrative promoted by jihadi groups in order to recruit foreign fighters highlights the continuous discrimination and marginalization of Muslims in Western societies, as well as the hostility toward Muslim countries, rather than specific religious imperatives to join the jihadi battle.[58] The intensification of tension between Muslim immigrant communities and the native population in many Western countries following 9/11 further facilitated the effectiveness of the jihadi propaganda and recruitment efforts.

In addition to tapping into identity politics, jihadi groups also seem to target vulnerable socioeconomic echelons of Western Muslim communities. Recent studies that gathered data about Western foreign fighters found that the majority didn't complete high school and less than 10 percent had an academic degree or were working in skilled occupations; thus, they are mostly students, unemployed, or working in temporary occupations that do not provide long-term career prospects.[59] No less importantly, the data also show that Western foreign fighters are more marginalized than other immigrants, including when compared to peers within their own communities. Overall, jihadi groups seemingly target young Westerners emerging from the lower socioeconomic echelons (even within their own immigrant communities) who lack opportunities for upward mobility and thus are open to adopting alternative lifestyles to improve their living conditions. This will stand in stark contrast to the broader population of terrorists discussed in the next chapter.

Interestingly, many Western foreign fighters are part of the same social networks (such as those based on family ties or shared residential areas). This is not necessarily surprising as past studies of social movements and terrorist groups have identified how peer pressure and inter-group dynamics within dense social networks might facilitate political radicalization and willingness to volunteer for suicide missions.[60] However, in this case, it seems that jihadi groups learned how to exploit such dynamics in a uniquely effective way and transformed specific towns and neighborhoods into reservoirs of (or perhaps incubators for) foreign fighters. Fairly small towns such as Vilvoorde and Molenbeek in Belgium, Ceuta in Spain, and Nice in France "exported" many foreign fighters, as jihadi recruiters were able to make inroads into the local Muslim communities.[61] More specifically, they exploited the fact that a decision of a single individual to join the jihadi struggle may, within a small and dense social network, lead to pressure on other members to imitate the same behavior, regardless of their level of commitment to or comprehension of the jihadi narrative and ideology.

## Vulnerabilities of Religious Terrorism

The rapid proliferation of religious terrorism in the last few decades created a sense that religious terrorist groups are inherently more competent, durable, and effective than past or other types of terrorist groups. This perception, or myth, masks a more complicated picture in which many religious terrorist groups fail to translate their battlefield achievements into political dividends as well as struggle to maintain a coherent ideological narrative.

Let's look again, for example, at the case of the Jewish terrorist groups, discussed above, that operated in the West Bank in the 1980s and 1990s. Despite some successful operations, both the Jewish Underground and the Bat-Ayin Underground never gained legitimacy with the Israeli public or mobilized significant support among the settler population from which they originated. Hence, in both cases the groups unsurprisingly failed to impact the political processes in Israel or to force policy changes (i.e., prevent peace negotiations between, for instance, Israel and Egypt and Israel and the Palestinians). Eventually, even most of the Jewish religious establishment condemned their actions.

Similarly, while the jihadi movement has proliferated around the globe, the movement has never managed to become the predominant religious doctrine in even one Muslim country, and still the great majority of Islamic scholars and leaders reject the violent path of radical jihadism. Moreover, as demonstrated earlier in this chapter, those Islamic groups that have endured and become politically influential have done so mainly because of their willingness to adopt nationalist/domestic ideas and not a global/religious dogma. Lastly, the Christian Identity movement has failed to become the predominant ideological stream even within the American Far Right and is still considered probably the smallest of the active white supremacy movements in the United States.

The failure of most religious groups to gain ideological and political prominence seems to result from two main characteristics of religious terrorism. The first is ideological inflexibility, which presents significant challenges in terms of both mass mobilization and adaptation to the changes in the geostrategic landscape. Ideological rigidity, which in many cases leads to operational conformism, is responsible for the relatively high rate of splits and intra-movement conflicts within militant religious movements. Because the ideological rigidity also limits the ability to gain political achievements via negotiations or conciliation processes, religious groups often corner themselves in a zero-sum framework, which undermines attempts to promote gradual progression toward fulfilling their goals.

The second characteristic is the limited mobilization potential of religious groups. While both left-wing and nationalist groups can potentially recruit and extract legitimacy from multiple ethnic, regional, and religious segments of the population, religious groups inherently limit their recruitment efforts to a very specific religious community. If that community is not the majority in the territory of operation, the group's ability to expand and to translate its violent operations into political achievements will remain limited. ISIS's ability to gain legitimacy among the Iraqi population was always limited to the Sunni areas of the country. Moreover, ISIS's tendency to perpetrate attacks against religious Shiite sites not only ensured the hostility of the Shiite Iraqi population but also led Iran to take an active role in the campaign against ISIS through sponsorship of local Iraqi Shiite militias.

## Concluding Remarks

This chapter deciphers some of the common myths and misconceptions about religious terrorism. We illustrate how religion or religiosity is not, in most cases, the primary facilitator of religious violence at either the collective or individual level. However, religion can help modern terrorists successfully organize. It is not required per se but certainly "greases the skids" of recruitment.[62] The religious orientation provides an overall advantage in social capital, or the benefits accruing to tight social networks. Members of a religious community are likely to stay loyal to other members of that community, are more accustomed to the lifestyle demands of adherence to the group religion, and share a set of supernatural beliefs. Thus, they make ideal recruits.[63] While the data clearly suggest that religion does not motivate terrorist activity, it certainly helps reduce the "costs of production" for terrorist groups.

This chapter also illustrates how despite the tendency to attach groups that promote religious violence with global aspirations, most focus more on the promotion of domestic, national campaigns and rarely operate outside their regional base. Again and again, we emphasize the importance of political preferences and dynamics in the proliferation of religious militancy and violence. These insights help us to develop a more rational picture of religious (and modern) terrorism. Now, we turn our attention to addressing other myths that continue to persist and hamper our ability to understand and more effectively combat terrorism.

## Notes

1. Hallenbeck 1991.
2. Hallenbeck 1991; Marine Corps Association, n.d.
3. Hiro 1993.
4. Baer 2002.
5. Friedman 1983.
6. Marine Corps Association, n.d.
7. Khatib, Matar, and Alshaer 2014; Hamzeh 2004; Leavitt 2015.
8. Laqueur 1999; Tan, Huat, and Ramakrishna 2002; Duyvesteyn 2004; Mockaitis 2008.
9. Gregg 2014; Khan 2011; Jones 2008; Gunning and Jackson 2011; Juergensmeyer 2013.
10. Perliger and Pedahzur 2014; Stern 2009; Juergensmeyer 2013.
11. Holtman 2005.
12. Ciment 1997.
13. Harik 2005; Worrall, Mabon, and Clubb 2015; Leavitt 2015.
14. Other groups, such as Hamas in the Palestinian territories and Al Shabab in Somalia, have provided social services as a way to garner local support.

15. Worrall, Mabon, and Clubb 2015; Avon, Khatchadourian, and Todd 2012; Hamieh and Ginty 2010.

16. Holtman 2005; Mishal and Sela 2006.

17. Chebab 2007; Biçakei 2007.

18. Hegghammer 2006.

19. Chelin 2018. Note that from a strategic perspective, ISIS and al-Qaeda likely do not seek material support from Boko-Haram or other affiliates but rather hope their existence will spread the demand for counterterrorism and therefore increase the costs to Western countries.

20. Coll 2004.

21. McMichael 2002; Bruce Amstutz 1994; Coll 2004.

22. Quarles 2004; Barkun 2014.

23. Perliger 2012a.

24. Perliger 2012a.

25. Sprinzak 1989.

26. Sprinzak 1989; Sprinzak 1991; Pedahzur and Perliger 2011.

27. Pedahzur and Perliger 2011.

28. Pedahzur and Perliger 2011.

29. Pedahzur and Perliger 2011.

30. Huntington 1996.

31. Avalos 2005; Kepel 2001; Norris and Inglehart 2002.

32. Bloom 2004; Enders and Sandler 2011; Pape 2003.

33. Cook 2008; Renard 2012.

34. Saud 2016.

35. Saud 2016; Inglehart and Norris 2009.

36. Kallis 2018.

37. Qureshi and Sells 2003.

38. Kellner 2002; Al-Obaidi, Abdullah, and Helfstein 2009; Ali 2003.

39. Jones, Smith, and Weeding 2003; Pedahzur and Perliger 2006; Sageman 2004.

40. Stern 2009; Toft 2007; Philpott 2013.

41. Post et al. 2016.

42. Whitehouse 2013; Wessinger 2009.

43. Cohen, Montoya, and Insko 2006.

44. Pape 2003.

45. Pape 2003, 2005.

46. Pape 2005.

47. de la Corte Ibáñez 2014; Pedahzur 2005; Merari 2010.

48. Pedahzur 2005. Note that many Middle Eastern and other organizations with "religious sounding" (typically "Arabic-sounding") names are actually leftist or nationalist organizations with little or no religious affiliation.

49. Perliger 2012a.

50. Perliger 2012a; Quarles 2004; Barkun 2014.

51. Perliger and Milton 2016.

52. Dickey 2014.

53. Lyons 2014.

54. Hegghammer 2006; Hegghammer 2013.

55. Mustapha 2013.

56. Byman and Shapiro 2014.

57. Perliger and Milton 2016.

58. Milton 2016.

59. Milton 2016; Perliger and Milton 2016.

60. Pedahzur and Perliger 2006.
61. Perliger and Milton 2016.
62. Berman 2003.
63. Iannaccone 2006.

4

# Myth: Terrorists Are Poor and Uneducated

*I fully believe the root cause of terrorism does come from situations where there is poverty, where there is ignorance, where people see no hope in their lives.*
—Colin Powell, former US secretary of state

*The war on terrorism will not be won until we have come to grips with the problem of poverty and thus the sources of discontent.*
—James Wolfensohn, former World Bank president

Much has changed in the wake of the terrorist attacks of September 11, 2001. At the same time that the United States organized multilateral coalitions to pursue terrorists with military and police forces, it also supported the international charge to eradicate the poverty that allegedly created terrorists. In the months following the attack, both liberal and conservative American leaders cast poverty and poor education as the most significant root causes of terrorism. Addressing the United Nations International Conference on Financing for Development in early 2002, then president George W. Bush stated, "We fight against poverty because hope is an answer for terror."[1] His predecessor, former president Bill Clinton, expressed similar views, calling terrorism the "dark side" of globalization and urging Americans to increase global security by helping to alleviate poverty.[2] And the international community also seemed convinced of this new framework for the eradication of the root causes of

47

terrorism. In 2002, UN Secretary-General Kofi Annan stated, "No one in this world can feel comfortable, or safe, while so many are suffering and deprived."[3] If liberals and conservatives around the world could agree on anything in the wake of 9/11, it was that ending poverty and increasing education would make the world safer. That sentiment persisted over time and across American governments. Speaking after meetings at the Vatican in 2014, former secretary of state John Kerry identified a "huge common interest in dealing with this issue of poverty, which in many cases is the root cause of terrorism."[4] In a recent speech, former Israeli president Shimon Peres put it plainly when he stated, "We must fight the causes of terrorism, which are poverty, ignorance."[5]

Almost immediately after 2001, world leaders turned their words into action. The near-universal consensus on the link between poverty and terrorism led to a tectonic shift in foreign aid distribution in the years that followed the 9/11 attacks. Within government and academic circles, connecting proposed poverty-alleviation projects to fighting terrorism significantly increased the likelihood of receiving funding. Official foreign aid surged to terrorism hotspots after 2001. Between 1996 and 2000, Iraq, Somalia, Sudan, and Syria together received about $1 billion in foreign aid per year. From 2002 to 2013, those countries took in approximately $9 billion in aid per year.[6] Pakistan provides perhaps the starkest example of US nonmilitary aid flowing to countries with desperately poor populations believed to be at risk for terrorist recruitment. As Figure 4.1 illustrates, in the ten years between 1992 and 2001, Pakistan received relatively little money from America's primary foreign aid agency, the United States Agency for International Development (USAID), with 1995 representing the peak year at $11 million. However, in the ten years from 2002 to 2011, Pakistan never received less than $288 million from USAID and reached a high-water mark of more than $1.3 billion in 2010. Clearly, the United States had shifted its foreign aid policy to address the threat of terrorism in the post-9/11 world.

Not just government leaders linked poverty, education, and terrorism. Nongovernmental organizations also beat the drum for making the world safer by making it less poor and more educated. The Bill and Melinda Gates Foundation has spent billions of dollars on alleviating poverty and increasing education since its establishment in 2000. While it would be unfair to say this foundation's purpose is to increase security, Bill Gates himself has repeatedly linked poverty and terrorism since September 2001. As recently as March 2017 in a *New York Times Magazine* piece, Gates castigated President Donald Trump's move to reduce foreign aid funding and projects. His simple answer to those

**Figure 4.1    US Agency for International Development Assistance to Pakistan, 1992–2011**

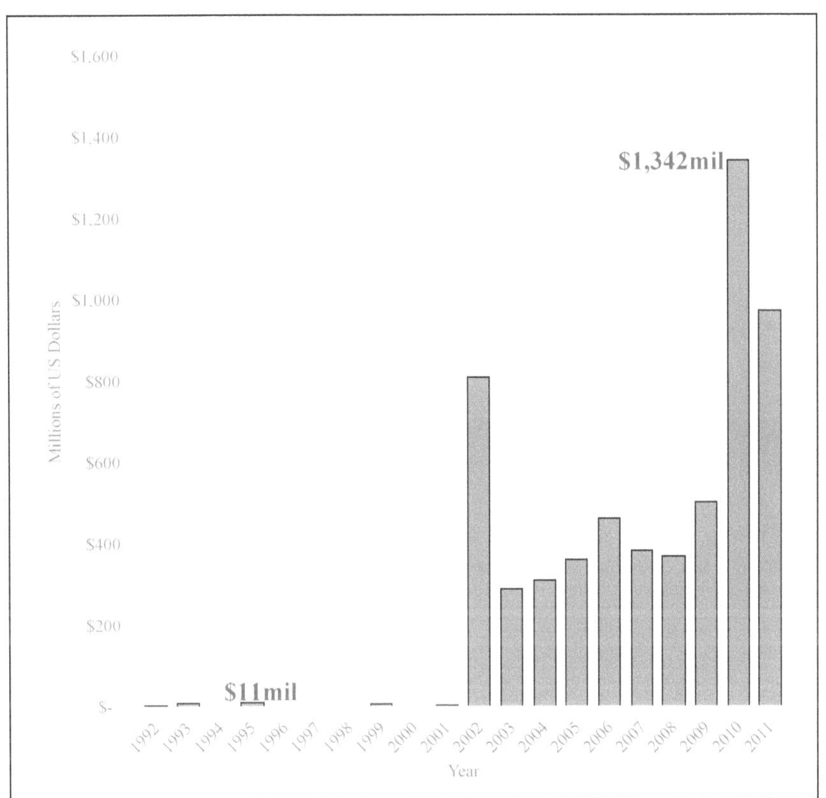


*Source:* USAID 2019.

who question the value of health and development programs around the world: "These projects keep Americans safe."[7]

The logic that "poverty and low education create terrorism" has strong appeal. We know an educated society is healthier and more productive.[8] Poverty also clearly causes suffering and humiliation for those it afflicts. It is easy to assume that poor, uneducated people, left behind by globalization and with few alternatives, are disenfranchised and more likely to be terrorists than wealthy, educated individuals. In fact, traditional rational-choice models used in fields such as economics might predict such a relationship similar to one that exists with crime.

Early work (which earned its author a Nobel Prize) sought to explain why poverty and crime are positively related. Criminals were viewed as rational and able to weigh the benefit of committing a crime versus the associated costs, such as risk of apprehension and punishment. Importantly for this discussion, poor potential criminals have a lower opportunity cost for committing any given crime and, therefore, are more likely to do so. It makes more sense for an unemployed, uneducated man to risk time in prison than it does for an individual with a steady job and future upward mobility opportunities to do so.[9] Similarly, a desperately poor young man with no prospects for a better future might more quickly resort to political violence, even terrorism, than his more educated, upwardly mobile countrymate.

Finally, we almost *want* terrorists to be poor and ignorant. Both poverty and poor education feel like issues the wealthy can and should do something about, especially if we believe doing so will make us safer. If the average global citizen feels generally helpless to stop terrorism, supporting poverty eradication and increased education feels like one of the few areas in which people can actually effect change. We essentially get a "two-for-one deal" if we can also make ourselves safer when we help decrease poverty and increase education. There is just one small problem: little evidence shows that either poverty or lack of education causes terrorism.

## Upon Further Examination

As appealing as it is, the conventional poverty-creates-terrorism wisdom has been countered with evidence over and over again in both academic and popular literature since before 9/11.[10] In the months and years that followed the attacks, article after article and book after book took this myth to task. Many authors, from *New York Times* op-ed contributors to the 9/11 Commission, pointed to perhaps the most obvious anecdotal evidence: the hijackers of September 11.[11] As it turned out, all the 9/11 attacks' pilots and planners had been enrolled in Western universities. Two-thirds of the twenty-five hijackers and planners involved had attended college.[12] And, of course, Osama bin Laden himself was a man of extreme wealth and privilege. As one *New York Times* contributor noted, "They were adults with education and skill, not hopeless young zealots. [They] spent . . . years studying and training in the United States, collecting valuable commercial skills and facing many opportunities to change their minds."[13]

As much as we might like to believe otherwise, nobody who played a significant role in the most devastating terrorist attack on American soil could be classified as either poor or uneducated. Most had the skills

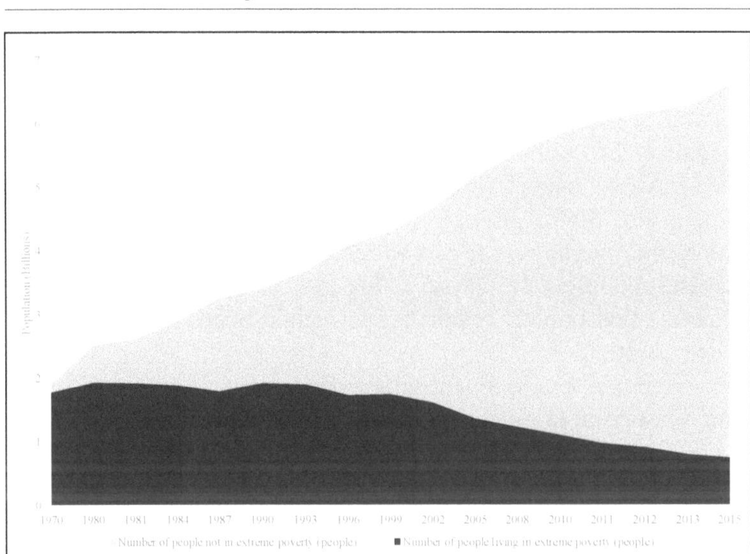

**Figure 4.2    The Number of People Living in Extreme Poverty and Not, 1970–2015**

*Source:* Authors, data acquired from *Our World in Data*, from World Bank Data.

The hypothesis, or myth, that poverty leads to terrorism has long been perplexing—largely, as discussed in this chapter, because there appears to be no evidence for it. From a very macro perspective, it is quite interesting to compare the trends in poverty with the trends in terrorism. Recall from Chapter 2 (Figure 2.1) that we have witnessed a marked rise in global terrorism since 1970, especially after 2004. This rise in terrorism coincides almost precisely with the relatively rapid drop in global poverty (Figure 4.2). Now, a correlation is not causation, but clearly the correlation between poverty on a global scale and terrorism on a global scale is negative. This ought to be the first indication that we should be skeptical of a claim that poverty leads to terrorism.

and opportunities to become successful professionals. Yet they chose a different path on which they would freely trade these opportunities for certain death and only a chance at changing the world they left behind.

But are the 9/11 attackers an anomaly, an exception to the rule that terrorists are poor and ignorant? To answer this question, we need to examine the existing larger body of knowledge and empirical data. We start with a seminal work focused on a number of different dimensions of terrorism and related topics, to include hate crimes, public opinion about violence in the West Bank and Gaza Strip, and the demographic makeup of Lebanese Hezbollah fighters, Palestinian suicide bombers, and Israeli Jews involved in terrorism. The researchers began with an investigation of public opinion about terrorist or militant activities directed toward Israel. Using polling data from the Palestinian Center for Policy and Survey Research (PCPSR), a nonprofit in Ramallah, Palestine, the researchers found widespread support for armed attacks against Israeli targets. However, as Figures 4.3 and 4.4 show, there was no evidence that public support for terrorism decreased with employment or education.[14]

For example, unemployed Palestinians were slightly less likely to support terrorism in pursuing political goals than almost all other employment categories. Similarly, support for terrorism was generally weaker among the illiterate population than among those with higher levels of education. In each area, the researchers found no evidence of a relationship between either poverty or education and terrorism. Or maybe more accurately, the little bit of relationship they did find actually indicated that terrorists, on average, were wealthier and more educated than the population from which they came.

Recognizing a significant leap from opinion to action, the researchers went on to examine the socioeconomic and educational status of Hezbollah fighters compared to the general Lebanese population in similar age groups. Drawing from biographical data for 129 members of Hezbollah's military wing who died in action from 1982 to 1994, the researchers found that while 33 percent of fifteen- to thirty-eight-year-old Lebanese lived in poverty during that time, the poverty rate for the Hezbollah fighters was only 28 percent. Figure 4.5 illustrates the point related to education.

Here, the education levels of Hezbollah fighters were compared to those of the general Lebanese population at the time. A much higher percentage of Hezbollah members had a secondary education in comparison to the general population, and a substantial percentage had undergraduate/graduate education.

**Figure 4.3    Results of December 12–24, 2001, PCPSR Poll of West Bank and Gaza Strip Public Support for Terrorist Activity by Occupation and Employment Status**

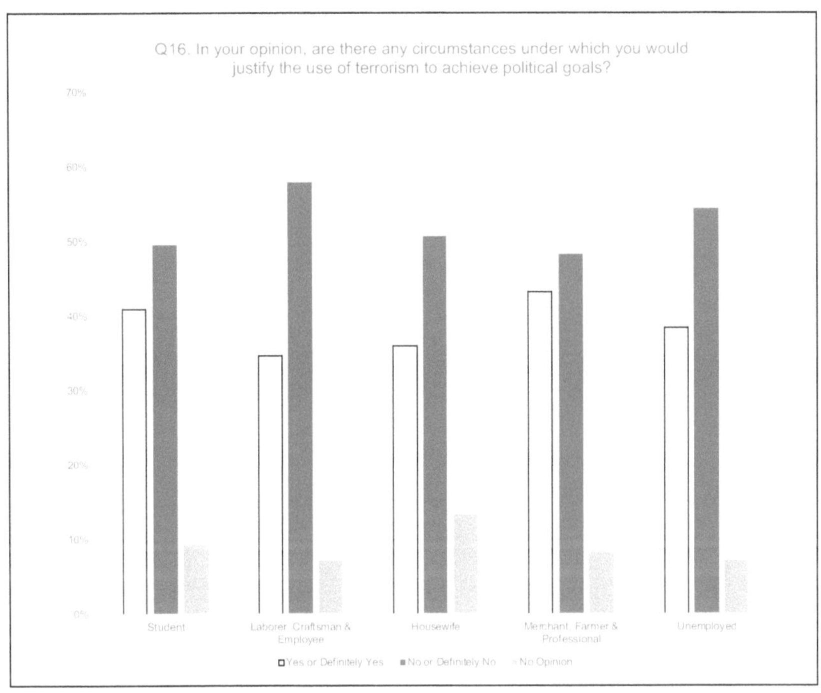


*Source:* Authors, data acquired from Krueger and Malečková 2003.

Subsequent work built on this seminal study by examining the link between poverty, education, and joining Hamas or the Palestinian Islamic Jihad (PIJ).[15] Biographical data reported on *shahid* (martyr) websites and other online journals of Hamas were used to compare the standard of living and education level of killed members of Hamas with those of the eighteen- to forty-one-year-old male Palestinian population from 1987 to 2002. As with Hezbollah fighters in Lebanon, this research found that deceased Hamas/PIJ members experienced a 16 percent poverty rate compared to a 31 percent poverty rate for Palestinians of similar age, sex, and religion. And while only 51 percent of the comparison population had achieved secondary education levels or higher, 96 percent of the Hamas/PIJ sample met this criterion. In fact, 56 percent

**Figure 4.4    Results of December 12–24, 2001, PCPSR Poll
of West Bank and Gaza Strip Public Support
for Terrorist Activity by Educational Attainment**

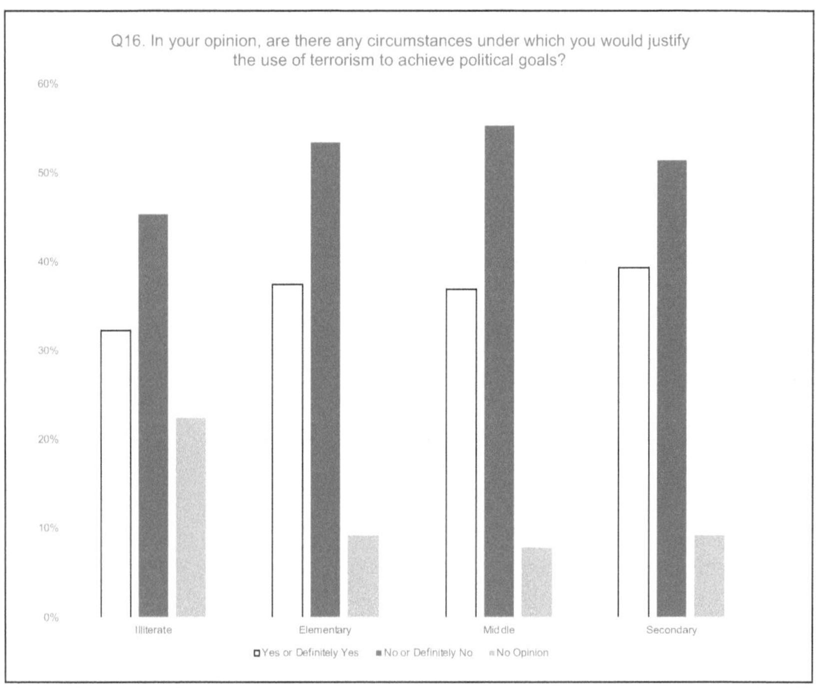


*Source:* Authors, data acquired from Krueger and Malečková 2003.

had attended postsecondary academic institutions. The findings not only failed to support the "poverty-causes-terrorism" trope but actually revealed a positive relationship between wealth, education, and death as a Hamas/PIJ suicide bomber.

While this research focused on the Middle East within a similar time window, research in other regions, focused on different times, comes to the similar conclusion that terrorists are typically not poor or uneducated. For example, one study utilized the profiles of over 350 individual terrorists active from 1966 to 1976.[16] Despite coming from countries as different as Argentina, Ireland, and Japan, approximately two-thirds had at least some university training, a rate much higher than found in the

**Figure 4.5    Education of Hezbollah Militants and Lebanese Population of Similar Age**

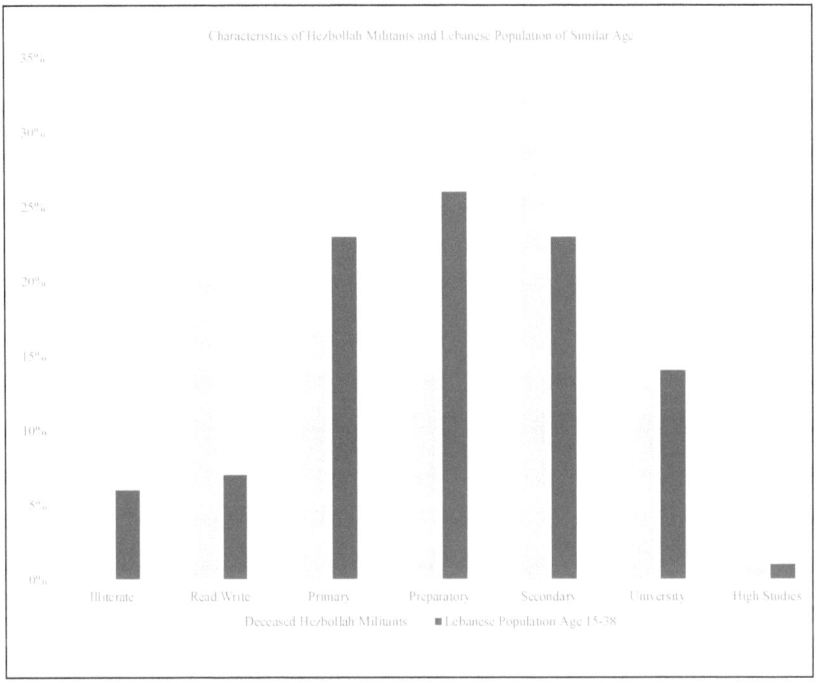

*Source:* Authors, data acquired from Krueger and Malečková 2003.

populations from which they came. Other research examined Cold War–era revolutionary movements and found the violent members were most often from the middle and upper classes. These groups spanned Europe (the German Baader-Meinhof Gang, the French Action Directe, and the Italian Red Brigades) and South America (Uruguay's Tupamaros, Nicaragua's Sandanistas, and Castro's Cuban revolutionaries).[17]

So the evidence seems clear: terrorists, on average, are not poor or uneducated. In fact, there may actually be a positive relationship between wealth, schooling, and terrorism. But why? To answer that question, we'll turn back to the field of economics. More specifically, thinking about the supply of and demand for terrorists can help us untangle the mess.

## Supply of Terrorists

As we consider the supply of individuals willing to become terrorists, it's helpful to remember the political aspect of our definition of terrorism.[18] If terrorism is in fact a violent means to achieve political goals, we should expect most terrorists to come from segments of the population that are typically most politically active. In America, like the rest of the world, income and political activity are highly correlated. When measured by voting, as shown in Figure 4.6, wealthier Americans consistently participate in the political process at much higher rates than do the poor.[19]

And this appears to be true over time as well. Going back at least thirty years, researchers could not find a single year in which voter turnout was higher for low earners than for high earners in the United States.[20] The fact that we see greater voting participation at higher income levels makes some sense. In inclusionary democratic systems, voting is an expression of preferences but also represents the means by which economic rents/benefits are allocated. Higher-income individuals have more to gain/lose in government distributions and, therefore, will most likely vote. And while poorer people have much to gain, they have less to lose in this process.[21]

Voting is one thing, though, and political activity to the point of violence, even suicide bombing, is another. Do we see similar breaks between the poor and wealthy when political activity becomes violent? Some historical data on violent and nonviolent political activists during India's anticolonial movement at the beginning of the twentieth century can help answer this question. In 1905, the British partitioned Bengal from India, hoping to create two manageable provinces while at the same time dividing Hindus and Muslims.[22] The decision, however, faced strong Indian opposition and ignited a self-rule movement previously unseen in India. It included large numbers of violent and nonviolent political activists, and the ruling government detained significant numbers of both types. Drawing on police records of Bengali agitation against the British-installed government, researchers have mapped out the demographics and socioeconomic status of the detainees, including their age, caste, occupation, income, and level of education. A comparison of all detained activists to the Bengali population yielded conclusive evidence that both the violent and the nonviolent political activists were significantly more educated and far richer than the population from which they came. For example, while less than 20 percent of the Bengali population could read, these activists averaged over fifteen years of schooling. The political activists were also much more likely to hold jobs in privileged sectors such as education, government, law, and medicine.

# Figure 4.6 American Voting Patterns by Household Income

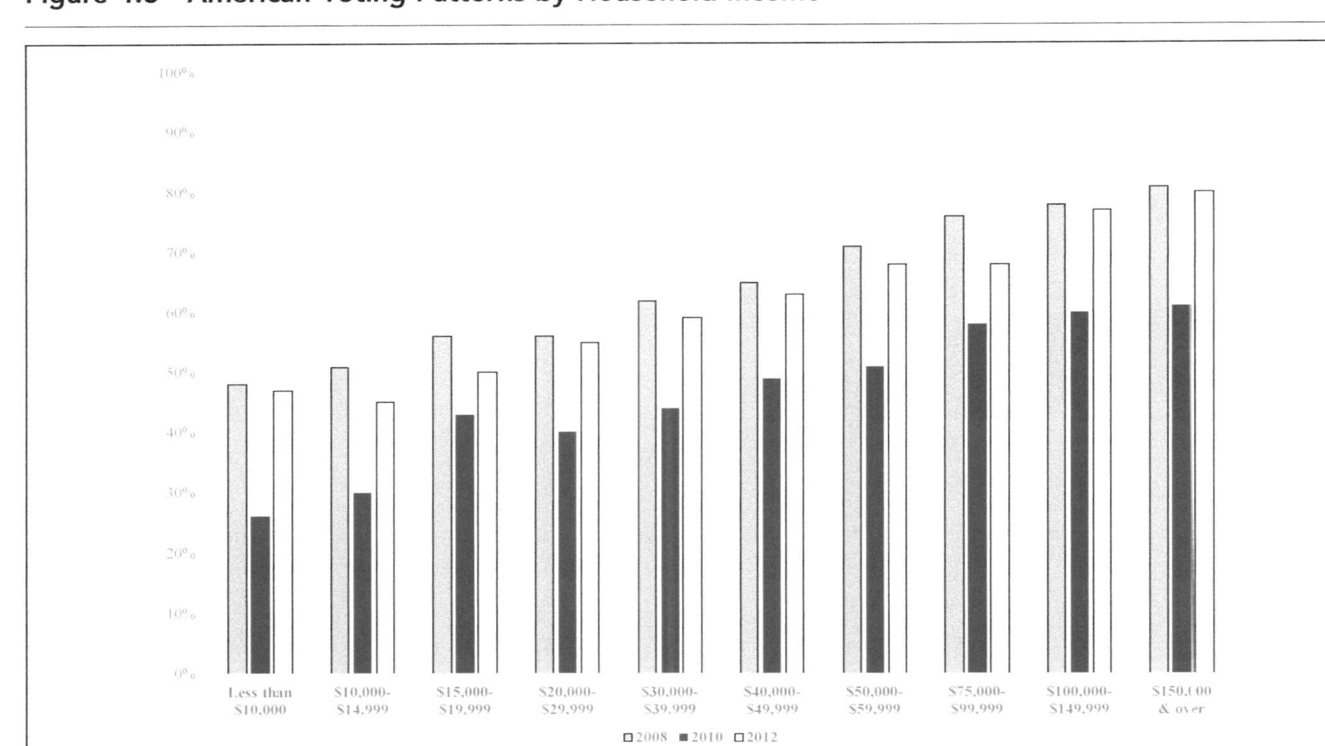


*Source:* Authors, data acquired from McElwee 2014.

While those comparisons are interesting, these data reveal something even more important for our purposes. Compared to nonviolent activists, violent activists (i.e., terrorists) were significantly less educated and poorer. The nonviolent activists had, on average, 2.3 years of additional schooling, earned more than 60 percent more per year in the labor market, and came from wealthier families. The terrorists, on the other hand, typically held lower-quality jobs compared to the nonviolent activists and were more likely to have failed national exams. Although better-off than the average citizen, the terrorists seem to be drawn from the bottom socioeconomic strata of the politically active class. What do we make of this?

These findings are critical as they begin to explain why the relationship between poverty, education, and terrorism may appear weak in the data. As Figure 4.7 highlights, the true relationship may not be linear but more like an inverted $U$.[23]

Although the exact mechanisms of terrorist supply are not known, the three regions shown in Figure 4.7 might provide some clarity. Region A represents the portion of the population that is relatively poor and uneducated (say the bottom third of the income distribution, for example). The empirical evidence indicates this segment is often not politically active in either violent or nonviolent ways. That is, they are neither activists nor significantly likely to vote/participate in political processes. In general, this group may be uninformed about the political process, maintain low expectations for change, or be unable to devote the time necessary to be politically active. Region C, conversely, represents the wealthiest and most educated portion of the population. These individuals are very politically active but less likely to engage in violence due to the opportunity cost of doing so. This is obviously not always the case (for example, consider Osama bin Laden), but the relationship generally holds true in the aggregate because people in this region are most likely in political power and have the most to lose from changing the status quo.

Region B, then, represents the segment of the population that is wealthy and educated enough to be politically active but not so much so as to be unwilling to take significant risk. People in this region have sufficient resources to attempt to effect change; they are most likely not in political power and could benefit substantially from a change in the status quo. But however well resourced, they (for any number of reasons) may not be capable of changing the status quo in nonviolent ways. Although no one individual is "likely" to become a terrorist, the data

**Figure 4.7    Hypothesized Relationship Between Wealth/
Education and the Probability of Being a Terrorist**

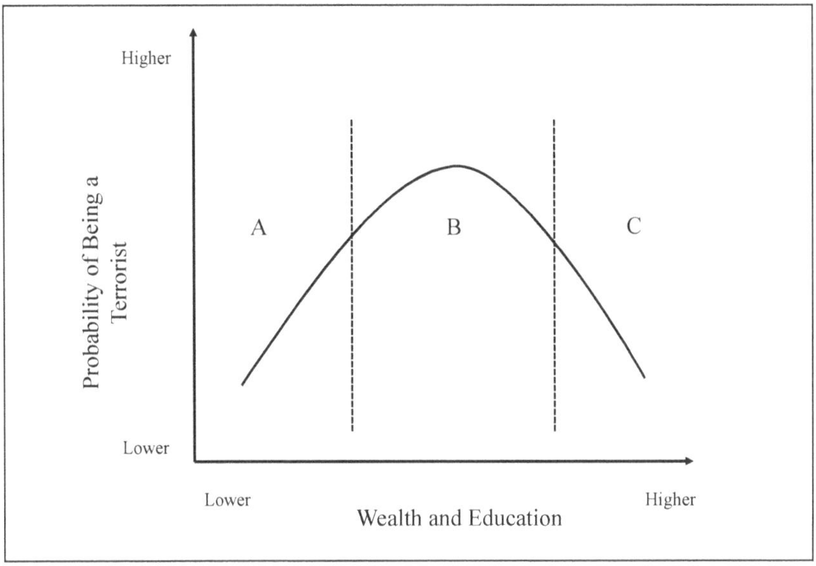

*Source:* Authors.

suggests that those who choose this path most often come from this group. The key finding here is that the suppliers of terrorism most likely are not poor and must be sufficiently educated and resourced to execute violence to effect political change.

## Demand for Terrorists

Supply is only half of the market. We cannot understand market outcomes without also considering demand, as the market for terrorists will not clear until supply equals demand. Thinking about the demand for terrorists seems strange until, again, we consider the political nature of the activity and the organizations that exist to achieve political outcomes. Political organizations must attract members to be effective, and the organizations that plan to use violence (i.e., terrorist organizations) must "hire" terrorists to do so. As long as there are more potential terrorists available than required (excess supply), organizations will have choice in who becomes a terrorist. This raises two questions: (1) Does the supply of terrorists exceed demand? and (2) Do terrorist organizations seek poor and uneducated workers?

A study of Hamas that included interviews with hundreds of the organization's activists, as well as family members of suicide bombers and even failed suicide bombers, found a clear surplus of willing terrorists.[24] The interviews reveal that Hamas leaders deliberated over which volunteers appeared most committed and likely to succeed. As one of those leaders indicated, "Our biggest problem is the hordes of young men who beat on our doors, clamoring to be sent. It is difficult to select only a few. Those whom we turn away return again and again, pleading to be accepted."[25]

ISIS seemingly faced a similar variant of this surplus-supply problem. As noted by bloggers from within the organization, many suicide bombers became frustrated by the length of time they had to wait for the opportunity to conduct an attack, blaming the delay on the backlog of volunteers. One purported Chechen ISIS member decried the long wait list and the nepotism that arose around it, writing, "Those Saudis have got things sewn up. They won't let anyone in. They are letting their relatives go to the front of the line and using 'blat' [connections]."[26]

So at least some evidence suggests that terrorist organizations can pick from an excess supply of potential terrorists. In a normal model of supply and demand in a labor market, when $S > D$, we expect to see a decline in price/wage. But another option is that, for any given price/wage, the labor demanders get to be pickier about labor quality. In that case, we would expect those organizations to choose the individuals most likely to accomplish their mission. On average, terrorist organizations should find individuals with more talent (skills, knowledge, and willingness) for terror more appealing, particularly for more difficult jobs. "One would hardly expect al-Qaeda to send some of its thousands of semi-literate mercenaries in Afghanistan to flight school in Florida if disaffected students in Europe were available."[27]

So, do we find evidence of talent-based selectivity in terrorist organizations? Not surprisingly, we do. One influential paper analyzed the demand for suicide bombers and found terrorist organizations faced high costs associated with incompetent or unreliable workers.[28] Unlike typical businesses, terrorist organizations face more than just the threat of going under—they are also exposed to potential detention or death.

These realities force the organization to create more complex internal structures and to reduce risk through detailed planning and redundancy. All these activities increase operating costs for the organization (a topic we address in more detail in Chapter 6). To lower these costs, terrorist organizations screen volunteers, typically selecting the more educated prospects. In a similar vein, others have pointed out that education may improve performance within a terrorist organization and in acts of terrorism, possibly because increased education creates a maturation effect.[29] Further, supply and demand dynamics facilitate the high proportion of engineers among jihadi groups.[30]

As we take a step back from the supply of and demand for terrorists, we should not be surprised to see how this market reaches equilibrium. Potential terrorists bring a set of skills and attributes to bear, and because supply outstrips demand, organizations have some power in choosing the "applicants" who best meet their needs. Just like in any complex organization in a labor market, we should expect leaders, organizers, and those filling the most demanding positions, such as suicide bombers or cross-border attackers, to be the most skilled and mature. As several prominent economists have noted, it is quite possible that highly qualified potential terrorists will volunteer only for the most important jobs, and terror organizations will select only the best for those jobs.[31] The market for terrorists, then, naturally reaches equilibrium when educated and skilled volunteers find organizations that need their talents.

This result does not mandate, however, that all terrorists or members of the organization be wealthy or college educated. For example, in Iraq during the height of insurgent activity, many of the more than 25,000 "terrorists" detained by the United States were poor and uneducated. In fact, because of their economic opportunities at the time, al-Qaeda's average monthly salary of $200 to $300 was enough to entice them to plant roadside bombs.[32] But these (mostly) men could hardly have been considered integral to the fight—they were essentially foot soldiers tasked with carrying out simple missions by more talented and educated leaders in the organization. We might visualize broader terrorism, then, as having a central core of wealthier, more educated leaders, planners, and executors of complex missions, with a periphery of "workers" who are more likely poorer and less educated.

But does all of this mean that poverty and lack of education have no bearing on the terrorism discussion? Not exactly. Several have championed poverty as furthering terrorism even if the individual terrorists are generally not poor or uneducated.[33] Most commonly, research looking for "root causes" of terrorism in poverty find instead that poverty and terrorism spring from a common well of broken institutions. We know that poor economic conditions often lead to an increase in political parties and activity.[34] The same government corruption and lack of rule of law that destroys economies also provides social revolutionaries a justification for their terrorist activities. These governments also commonly fail to provide civil liberties to their citizens, preventing nonviolent dissent and provoking violent protest. When researchers control for levels of civil liberties, per capita income does not predict the production of terrorism.[35] Because of this, policies that address broken institutions are likely to address poverty and terrorism simultaneously.[36]

## Concluding Remarks

Contrary to the passionate speeches and well-intended policies made by world leaders since 2001, the evidence is clear: terrorists are typically neither poor nor ignorant. In fact, the average terrorist is more educated than the population from which he or she comes. Terrorists are not terrorists because they are desperate and have no better option. Rather, circumstances other than economic well-being likely drive the choice to become a terrorist. Other, perhaps correlated, motivations appear to be at work here.

So should we end all poverty-alleviation efforts around the world and start bombing schools? No, but we may want to reconsider our current approach to counterterrorism. Pouring more foreign aid into governments with broken institutions will not likely reduce terrorism—it may actually have the opposite effect. In fact, the only policies likely to reduce the demand for terrorism (and the requisite supply to meet it) are those that lead to better institutions in currently broken systems and thereby lessen the perceived marginal benefits of engaging in terrorism in the first place. This is not to say that supply-side efforts to increase the cost of supplying terrorism are worthless either. Interdicting financing sources, military and law enforcement operations, increased security measures, and so forth, may all "shift the supply" of terrorism to the left. But, as illustrated in this chapter, attempts to impact the "demand" side of the market are likely missing their mark. Subsequent chapters continue to address these issues. We cover further implications for counterterrorism in later sections of this book, but for now remember this: terrorists are neither poor nor ignorant.

## Notes

1. Bush 2002.
2. Watanabe 2002.
3. Annan 2002.
4. Bier 2014.
5. Peres 2015.
6. Easterly 2017.
7. Gates 2017.
8. Becker 1962.
9. Becker 1968.
10. Russell and Miller 1983.
11. Bergen and Pandey 2005; Kean 2011.
12. Bergen and Pandey 2005.
13. Wilgoren 2001.
14. Krueger and Malečková 2003.
15. Berrebi 2007.
16. Russell and Miller 1983.
17. Radu 2004.
18. Others explain this phenomenon by considering hate crimes, a close cousin of terrorist activity. Although Becker's findings on the relationship between property crime and poverty still hold, there is no evidence that hate crimes are more likely to be committed by poor, uneducated people. Krueger and Malečková 2003.
19. McElwee 2014. Interestingly, one of the most famous American terrorist organizations, the Weather Underground, was composed of highly educated Ivy League students.
20. Franko and Kelly 2016.
21. Frey 1971.
22. Lee 2011.
23. Of course, if we used a straight line to approximate this relationship, it would have a slope of zero, indicating no relationship between wealth, education, and terrorism.
24. Hassan 2001.
25. Hassan 2001.
26. Mastracci 2015.
27. Berman 2003.
28. Iannaccone 2006.
29. Benmelech and Berrebi 2007.
30. Gambeta and Hertog 2016.
31. Buendo de Mesquita 2005; Becker 2005.
32. Azarva 2009.
33. Becker 2005; Buendo de Mesquita 2005.
34. Alesina, Ozler, and Swagel 1996.
35. Krueger and Laitin 2008.
36. Post et al. 2016.

# 5

# Myth: Terrorists Are Crazy

After 9/11, it was common to read a newspaper article or hear on the nightly news about "crazy" terrorists attacking America, and the headlines continue today. For example, a *New York Times* headline on July 25, 2018, read, "Toronto Shooting Rekindles Familiar Debate: Terrorist? Mentally Ill? Both?"[1] This headline and anecdotal evidence highlight the common lay belief that terrorists are mentally ill. Defining terrorists as "crazy" is appealing, as explaining why a person willingly flew a plane into a building, killing thousands of people, is much easier if he suffered from some mental disorder. It is significantly more troubling to consider that a "normal" person took a calculated and rational approach to committing mass murder. However, just because it is easy and comforting to label terrorists as "crazy" does not mean that all, or even most, suffer from a mental disorder. This chapter discusses the research examining the relationship between terrorism and mental illness. It then explores psychological research that has attempted to explain and predict why people would join a terrorist organization or commit a terrorist act. The chapter concludes with a look at how uncertainty-identity theory can explain and define individuals' involvement in terrorist activities.

## Upon Further Review: Are Terrorists Crazy?

Answering the question "Are terrorists crazy?" is a bit more complicated than one may think. First, *crazy* is not a clinical term according to the American Psychiatric Association's *Diagnostic and Statistical Manual of Mental Disorders* (*DSM*).[2] Additionally, even using the *DSM*, answering this question is difficult because mental disorders for terrorists could fall under one of two major classifications: major clinical illness or personality disorder. The major distinction between clinical illness (i.e., psychosis or psychopathy) and personality disorder (i.e., sociopathy) is that sociopaths know right from wrong, whereas psychopaths do not. That is, a person suffering from mental illness does not possess the ability to determine right from wrong (or the appropriate behavior in a situation), whereas people suffering from a personality disorder know right from wrong but choose to do the wrong thing anyway.

The research on clinical illness and terrorism is sparse—and for good reason: it is very difficult to conduct a comprehensive psychological examination of a terrorist in a controlled research environment. Thus, research has been conducted in the field and under less than ideal settings. Results from this work suggest that terrorists usually do not have diagnosable clinical illnesses.[3] For example, researchers, using the *DSM*, psychologically evaluated members of the Baader-Meinof Gang[4] and a radical Islamic Middle Eastern terrorist group[5] and found no diagnosable mental illnesses across the individuals examined. Given that the longer arc of research over decades has found that few terrorists suffer from clinical mental illness,[6] we can most likely set it aside as a root cause of terrorism.

By contrast, an abundance of research examines the relationship between personality disorders and terrorism, with the majority focusing on terrorists' antisocial behaviors. Antisocial behaviors are a trademark of certain personality disorders (e.g., antisocial personality disorder, sociopathy[7]). For example, researchers propose that terrorists have a personality disorder manifest in their values and ruthlessness,[8] and, surprisingly, some researchers argue that the types of tattoos terrorists have back up the claim that they suffer from personality disorders.[9] However, these arguments do not stand up to further scrutiny. For example, terrorists, it is often hypothesized, conduct terrorist acts on behalf of their terrorist organization[10] or to help obtain food/safety for their families. A person suffering from antisocial personality disorder does not engage in behaviors on behalf of or out of concern for other people.[11] In fact, a key characteristic of the antisocial personality is a lack of empathy (not caring about other people), and while terrorists may not care about you based on your group membership (e.g., your being an American), they do care about their groups or their families. Thus, the argument that terrorists suffer from antisocial personality disorders does not seem to hold up to logic and data.[12] Recent data does suggest, however, that lone actors (e.g., people who work and act by themselves to cause terror, such as school shooters) do suffer from mental disorders.[13]

The search for a common "terrorist personality" has been equally unsuccessful to this point. Research on terrorist organizations, such as the Italian Red Army Brigades or the Basque Euskadi Ta Askatasuna, uncovered no personality traits consistent across members.[14] Other researchers suggest that pathological personality defects as a result of negative early life experiences can lead a person to develop a negative view of authority figures and to become a terrorist.[15] Several personality-defect models propose various personality types. For example, some researchers suggest that humiliation during childhood leads to the development of a pathological need to aggress against authority.[16] Other research details two personality-defect types, the anarchic-ideologue and the nationalist-secessionist.[17] Still others propose three personality-defect types: the leader, the opportunist, and the idealist.[18] The personality-defect models enjoy only minimal support, and the majority of the work is theoretical and has never been tested.[19] However, recent research suggests that suicide bombers have different personality traits than other members of terrorist organizations.[20] For example, suicide bombers have more avoidant-dependent personality disorders and display more suicidal tendencies and depressive symptoms.[21]

Overall, the currently available data simply do not support the idea that terrorists are "crazy," or suffer from a mental illness or personality disorder. While the personality-defect approach to explaining terrorism has minimal support, that work requires significantly more research. Additionally, work on personality suggest that at most (under ideal scenarios) personality traits explain less than 50 percent of behavior.[22] In other words, even the best personality-trait models cannot tell us why most people do what they do. Does the broader field offer any other hope for explaining the psychology of a terrorist?

## Other Approaches to Explain Terrorism

Beyond the mental illness and personality disorder approach to explain terrorism, several other researchers have attempted to explain and predict terrorism using well-established theories from psychology. The main theories outlined below have sequentially been proposed with only limited empirical backing. We also discuss a more promising line of thinking about why people become terrorists from a psychological perspective.

## Social Learning Theory

Psychologists developed social learning theory[23] to explain how people learn by watching others. In the famous bobo doll study,[24] researchers had children watch a video of an adult playing with a bobo doll in either a nonaggressive or aggressive manner. Next, children were placed in a room full of toys, one of which was the bobo doll, and the researchers observed that those children who watched the aggressive video were significantly more likely to play aggressively (particularly with the bobo doll) compared to those who watched the nonaggressive video. These results indicate that aggression is learned from watching other people (especially authority figures). These studies suggest that aggressiveness is not just a genetic personality trait but also can be acquired via learning. This theory has emotional appeal: after all, we do not want to be thought of as predestined to terrorism and we like to believe that learned behavior can be changed.

Some researchers have suggested that engaging in terrorist activities is a learned behavior.[25] For example, some argue that exposure to glorification of violence influences teens living in dangerous/highly violent regions of the world to join militant groups.[26] Others suggest that support for and a tendency to engage in political violence result from learning and indoctrination in extreme religious educational institutions, such as in many Pakistani or Palestinian madrasas or schools for young boys.[27] Thus, some data show that terrorist indoctrination, or learning to see a specific group as the target, may be effective for breeding individuals (e.g., future terrorists) who will propagate those messages and actions. Additionally, terrorist-related propaganda is now mass distributed online and is available across social media platforms (e.g., ISIS created a massive online infrastructure in order to utilize Facebook, twitter, and so forth to disseminate its ideology and recruit new members). Given, the plethora of opportunities to learn about terrorism and become a terrorist in some regions of the world, the social learning approach to explaining terrorism appears to have logical and even emotional merit. However, when one examines the regions of the world where terrorism is glorified, only a small percentage of the population actually engages in terrorism. Hence, social learning seems able to explain only a small portion of what motivates a person to join a terrorist organization. For example, during the high days of the Palestinian Al-Aqsa uprising, posters depicting and glorifying martyrs who conducted suicide attacks flooded Palestinian refugee camps; however, only a small portion of terrorists were recruited from those refugee camps.[28] So social learning theory has limited merit in explaining what motivates terrorism.

### Frustration Aggression Hypothesis

The frustration aggression hypothesis[29] is the most widely studied theory that predicts when people will aggress against others. The premise is rather simple: the root cause of aggression is frustration; thus, to aggress, someone must first become frustrated. According to this theory, people are motivated to join a terrorist organization as a result of growing frustration with their situation or that of their community/nation. Ted Gurr's (1970) relative deprivation theory further argues that the widening gap between people's expectations and the political reality is the main source of frustration in the context of politically motivated violence. Unfortunately, the application of the frustration aggression hypothesis to terrorism suffers from similar pitfalls as the social learning theory. Many people in terrorism-prone regions are frustrated (often understandably so) but never join terrorist organizations, and several terrorist organizations have been created by and are filled with people from privileged backgrounds who have no reason to be frustrated (e.g., the leftist terrorist groups in Europe during the 1970s[30]). The frustration aggression hypothesis explains only a small portion of what motivates people to join terrorist organizations.

### Terror Management Theory

Terror management theory (TMT)[31] argues that people experience "paralyzing terror" when they think about their own mortality. To adapt to and overcome this potential terror, humans create and maintain a meaningful, orderly, and consistent conception of the world—commonly referred to as a cultural worldview.[32] Cultural worldviews help humans overcome the potential terror associated with their own deaths by making them believe their lives are significant and enduring and by providing them with a positive view of themselves.[33]

One way in which humans infer that their lives have meaning is through literal immortality seeking, which can involve belief in an afterlife or observance of religious rituals.[34] Another, more common method for inferring that life has meaning is by increasing connections with cultural institutions that promote and confirm the individual's worldview and promote self-esteem—referred to as symbolic immortality seeking. TMT is one of the most widely researched theories in social psychology, having inspired more than 350 studies in at least fifteen countries.[35] Not surprisingly, research on TMT has expanded to account for gaps in other literatures and theories—for instance, research examining mortality salience (thinking about death) and support for terrorism and terrorist activities.[36] Results from studies conducted in Iran and the United States suggested that mortality salience increased support for terrorism for Iranians; however, for Americans, mortality salience increased support for counterterrorism. Thus, mortality salience is not a consistent predictor of support for or joining a terrorist organization, but it may play a role in some contexts.

### Significance Quest Theory

According to significance quest theory (SQT) people have a fundamental need for meaning in their lives, and when denied it, they act to restore it.[37] One possible method to restore meaning in life, according to SQT, is to join and support terrorist organizations. Testing SQT, researchers found that refugees from Iraq and Palestine reported greater life meaning the more they were willing to sacrifice their lives for a cause.[38] Additionally, the same researchers found that experimentally manipulating people to feel less meaning in life led to greater willingness to sacrifice the self, and having people recall a time they self-sacrificed led to a sense of greater meaning in life. Thus, people who feel like their lives have no meaning can turn to terrorist organizations to find fulfillment. Additionally, one could see terrorist organizations as threatening members' sense of meaning in life in order to get them to self-sacrifice for the group (e.g., suicide bombers). However, a lot of work on SQT remains before we can understand the role that meaning in life plays in motivating people to join terrorist organizations in the real world.

### Sensation Seeking

Sensation seeking[39] is an individual personality trait related to seeking and enjoying highly stimulating activities (e.g., illicit drug use, sky diving). Scholars have argued that people join terrorist organizations so that they can engage in thrilling and exciting social movements.[40] The United Nations has suggested that the excitement of joining a social movement explained why young people traveled from around the world to join

ISIS.[41] On the empirical side, one researcher conducted a survey of incarcerated violent extremists and found that they reported excitement as a main motivator for joining extremist groups.[42] Recently, other researchers integrated sensation seeking into the significance quest theory, proposing that sensation seeking explains why those who seek meaning in life support and join terrorist organizations.[43] Across several experiments B. Schumpe and colleagues found that those with heightened need for meaning in life experienced greater sensation seeking and that increased sensation seeking was strongly associated with support for political violence. Taken together, all the work indicates that people who score high in sensation seeking are at risk for joining terrorist organizations. However, not all terrorists evince high levels of sensation seeking.

### Right-Wing Authoritarianism and Social Dominance Orientation

Right-wing authoritarianism (RWA) and social dominance orientation (SDO) are strong predictors of prejudice, discrimination, and intergroup violence.[44] RWA refers to a tendency to submit to authority, a desire to see the behavior of others controlled through the threat of punishment, and a strong commitment to social norms and traditions.[45] SDO refers to a general preference for intergroup hierarchies, where high SDO is associated with a desire for intergroup relations to be arranged according to distinctions of superiority and inferiority.[46] Scoring high in both RWA and SDO has been related to greater prejudice against women[47] and black Americans,[48] support for restrictive policies against members of the LGBTQ community,[49] and, most importantly, support for terrorism.[50] To date, only a single study that surveyed people in America and Lebanon examines the correlation between SDO, RWA, and terrorism. Thus, more work is needed to understand the role that SDO and RWA play in terrorism.

### Cognitive Styles

Cognitive styles refer to the ways that people think about the world around them (including potential prejudices and attribution biases). Past research has linked how people think about violence and aggression,[51] and this led some researchers to propose that the way some people think may lead them to join terrorist organizations.[52] For example, some researchers suggest that people who join terrorist groups suffer from a fundamental attribution error: thinking that the hated group is evil and deserves destruction.[53] To date, this idea has not been tested; nor does it explain why a person would identify with the terrorist organization in the first place, unless the fundamental attribution error occurred before the individual joined the group, but that is unlikely. Other cognitive styles proposed to predict terrorism[54] include the need for closure (i.e., to think one has answers and to think about the world simply, in black and white or in terms of good versus evil),[55] the need for cognition,[56] and the need for conceptual or integrative complexity.[57] Overall, there is little research to suggest that cognitive styles predict people's willingness to join terrorist organizations.[58]

## Other Theoretical Approaches

Beyond the theories discussed above, several other theories from social psychology have been applied or adapted to explain individuals' involvement in terrorist activities. These include, but are not limited to, collectivism, rational choice theory, oppression theory, and identity theory.[59] Across the applications of these theories, there is some evidence that supports[60] and some evidence that does not support the application to terrorism.[61] Many need to be tested (e.g., identity theory), and, overall, no consistent evidence in the literature supports large-scale adoption of one of the theories to predict or explain involvement in terrorism (see Table 5.1).

## Table 5.1   Theories That Predict Terrorism

| Theory | Prediction | Support |
| --- | --- | --- |
| *Major clinical illness* | Major clinical illness (e.g., depression) causes people to join a terrorist organization. | None |
| *Personality disorder* | Personality disorders (e.g., borderline personality disorder) cause people to join a terrorist organization. | None |
| *Personality types* | People with certain personality types (e.g., the terrorist personality) are most likely to join terrorist organizations. | None |

*continues*

**Table 5.1 Continued**

| Theory | Prediction | Support |
|---|---|---|
| *Social learning theory* | People learn to become terrorists by watching other terrorists and learning terrorism from television or in religious writings. | Partial support |
| *Frustration aggression hypothesis* | People are motivated to join a terrorist organization because they are frustrated with their life situations. | Partial support |
| *Relative deprivation* | People who experience relative deprivation feel humiliated and discriminated against, and these feelings motivate them to join a terrorist organization. | Partial support |
| *Terror management theory* | Mortality salience (thinking about one's death) motivates people to support terrorist organizations that protect against or assuage fear of death. | Partial support |
| *Significance quest theory* | People who lack meaning in their lives can meet that need by joining a terrorist organization. | Partial support |
| *Sensation seeking* | People with high levels of sensation seeking join terrorist organizations to engage in thrilling and exciting social movements. | Partial support |
| *RWA and SDO* | People who score high in RWA and SDO are more likely to support and join terrorist organizations. | Little support |
| *Cognitive styles* | The way people think can lead them to join a terrorist organization. | None |
| *Uncertainty identity theory* | People identify with terrorist organizations to reduce uncertainty about themselves, their futures, or their place in the world. | Good support |

## *A New Approach to Explain Terrorism: Uncertainty*

Societal instability and uncertainty (e.g., government instability or uncertainty about access to food, security, etc.) seem to precede the rise of terrorist organizations.[62] For example, a factor contributing to the creation of ISIS was instability and uncertainty surrounding political and government changes in Iraq after the Iraq War.[63] ISIS capitalized on the instability and uncertainty to create a large terrorist organization (which desired to become a state or caliphate) that killed thousands of people and created a worldwide terror network in the 2010s. Similarly, the Taliban capitalized on instability and governmental uncertainty in Afghanistan in the early 1990s to advance its political agenda and engage in violent activities against the Afghan government, until it was able to take control of most of the country in 1996. In the United States, terrorist organizations formed in the context of social and political instability (e.g., the Ku Klux Klan to combat social equality for African Americans during the Reconstruction and civil rights eras). Across these examples and the many others that we could list here, social instability or uncertainty is a common thread facilitating the emergence of the terrorist organization. An important question is why instability or uncertainty would lead to the creation of, and motivate people to join, terrorist organizations.

One idea is that people are motivated to identify with groups out of an epistemic need to reduce self-uncertainties.[64] A basic motive that drives people is the desire to understand and be able to make predictions about their worlds. Not knowing or being uncertain about one's self or one's place in the world is highly uncomfortable and sets in motion behaviors aimed at reducing that uncertainty. This is not to say that all self-uncertainties are aversive and viewed as a threat. Some uncertainties can serve as challenges that provide people with satisfaction when they are overcome; consider the sky diver who jumps out of a plane with a parachute for the thrill. However, uncertainty can be highly anxiety provoking and make us feel powerless to control our world because we are unable to plan for the future. Living in a terrorism-prone region of the world (or an area of poor governance), where access to food, safety, and other basic life necessities is unpredictable, raises uncertainty in an aversive way and motivates people to reduce those uncertainties.

Feelings of uncertainty motivate people to identify with social groups that reduce, control, or protect an individual from feelings of uncertainty. The process of identifying with a group reduces uncertainty by providing a view of the world that tells us who we are and how we should behave; it gives the individual immediate acceptance and validation. For example, college freshmen commonly experience high levels of uncertainty (often because they are unsure about their new environment, who their friends are, how they fit in, etc.), which motivates them to seek out and identify with groups on campus (e.g., sororities and fraternities). These groups tell members exactly how to think, feel, and behave, and thereby reduce their uncertainty.

Once people identify with a group, they no longer think of themselves as unique individuals and attempt to adopt and follow the norms of the group.[65] So, by extension, if people live in an area with uncertainty about where they will get their next meal or about their personal safety, they can identify with a terrorist group to help them feed and protect themselves and their families, thereby resolving those uncertainties. A consequence of identifying with a group to reduce uncertainty is that members will strongly adhere to the group's norms. Thus, once people identify with a terrorist group to reduce uncertainty, they will strongly uphold and protect that group and its values and beliefs.

Highly homogenous, or "entitative,"[66] groups are particularly well equipped to reduce self-uncertainty. Highly entitative groups tell people exactly how to think, feel, look, and behave, and these strict norms do a very good job of reducing uncertainty. Fraternity and sorority members, church members, members of athletic teams, and so forth, often dress alike, read similar books, and listen to the same music. Membership entails adoption of similar habits and also often leads to "groupthink," or the tendency to hold the same opinions as the group.

Under uncertainty, people prefer to identify with highly entitative groups, tend to identify more strongly with them, and seek to make more entitative those groups to which they already belong.[67] With an increase in entitativity comes an increase in adherence to norms. In this way norms provide members with a clear sense of who they are, what they should believe, and how they should behave.[68] The more people feel like they fit in with the group, or the extent to which they believe they meet group norms, the less uncertain they feel. Thus, by following group norms, people reduce uncertainty. Terrorist groups tend to be very high in entitativity and have very clear rules about exactly how people should think, feel, and behave; for example, the madrasa (religious school for Muslim boys) is based on Islamic fundamentalism and has very strict rules for behavior.[69] This makes joining terrorist organizations a potentially effective tool for reducing uncertainty since many of them provide their members with a clear normative framework, including behavioral practices that they are supposed to follow.

An interesting question is whether a terrorist organization could create uncertainty in its environment (via terrorist attacks, for instance) and then use that uncertainty to get people to join the organization. A bit of research supports that idea: researchers had group leaders increase uncertainty (or certainty) among followers and then measured how strongly the latter identified with the group. Results demonstrated that leaders who increased uncertainty in their followers increased identification with the group, while increasing certainty in followers did not impact identification.[70] This work suggests that terrorist organizations may be able to create uncertainty via their activities and then capitalize on that uncertainty by getting people to join their organization. Future research is needed to assess that idea.

There now exists a large base of literature demonstrating that uncertainty motivates people to identify with a group, particularly an extremist group, to reduce uncertainty.[71] For example, researchers examined the impact of uncertainty on radicalism at a college campus.[72] Participants watched a video of a student leader of an ostensible student group, and the group was described using either extremist or moderate language. After watching the video, participants had their uncertainty about the future manipulated by the experimenter to be high or low. Results demonstrated that participants high in uncertainty were significantly more likely to identify with the extremist group compared to the moderate group, whereas those low in uncertainty were more likely to identify with the moderate group. Other research has replicated these results using a similar population, finding that uncertainty motivated identification with the radical group.

Additionally, researchers examined the impact of uncertainty on support for extremism in the Middle East.[73] This study examined how uncertainty and national identity (with Israel or Palestine) interacted to predict the promotion of extremist actions to protect one's country. The results confirmed predictions—people who most strongly identified with their country and were uncertain were the most likely to endorse extremist behaviors to protect their country. Finally, researchers examined the relationship between uncertainty and support for extreme behavior.[74] Their results demonstrated that those who felt like they did not fit in (which increases self-uncertainty[75]) thought that engaging in extreme behaviors would make group members more likely to accept them. These results indicate that leaders can make members feel like they do not fit in with the group to get them to engage in extreme behaviors. Overall, this work demonstrates that uncertainty is a clear motivator for people to identify with extremist groups (e.g., a terrorist organizations) and commit or endorse extremist behaviors. However, the link between uncertainty and terrorism is limited to a single study, so more replication is needed.

Recent research suggests that beyond motivating people to identify with extremist groups, uncertainty may play a pivotal role in motivating groups to attack after they have been threatened. Here, research examined the role that uncertainty and threat play in willingness to retaliate against the threatening group.[76] Two different studies showed that when their group is threatened, people experience an increase in uncertainty, and that uncertainty motivates them to retaliate against/attack the threatening group (a subject considered again in Chapter 7). A follow-up study demonstrated that not only does threat cause people to retaliate and attack the threatening group, but group members are also willing to endure physical pain for their group.[77]

Feeling uncertain about one's self or one's surroundings is linked to defensive strategies and intergroup conflict. For example, individuals who possess high chronic uncertainty, such as those who try to avoid uncertainty at all costs, perceive out-groups as more threatening[78] and hold more prejudice against groups that differ in defined core values.[79] The uncertainty management model[80] demonstrates that uncertainty motivates individuals to defend their worldviews and personal convictions,[81] define other groups in derogatory ways, exhibit willingness to die for their religious views, and support war to defend religious beliefs.[82] Clearly, evidence is growing that uncertainty is a powerful motivator, particularly of extremist and terrorism-related behaviors.

Uncertainty motivates people to identify with groups, particularly highly entitative groups (such as terrorist organizations), as well as to support extreme positions in the group, retaliate against groups that threaten them, and take risks for the group, even putting themselves in harm's way. An important implication of all this work is that uncertainty may be a driver of terrorist activities. When outside groups (e.g., the American government or another religious, ethnic, or political group) threaten terrorist organizations, their members experience an increase in uncertainty. Psychologically, attacking members of the threatening group reduces that uncertainty. One implication is that working on dealing with social instability and uncertainty, as opposed to attacking terrorist groups, may be more productive in reducing the "demand" for terrorism in the first place. However, we are in the early stages of assessing the role that uncertainty plays in terrorism. Future research is needed to tease apart the causal link between uncertainty and retaliatory behavior, and the research needs to extend beyond laboratory studies and examine real terrorist organizations and their members.

## Concluding Remarks

When a terrorist attack occurs, the news often reports that the perpetrator must be crazy or suffering from a mental illness. Clearly, a common lay belief is that terrorists are mentally ill. Defining terrorists as "crazy" is appealing, as explaining why a person would willingly become a suicide bomber is much easier if he or she suffers from some mental disorder. It is significantly more troubling to consider that a "normal" person has taken a calculated and rational approach to killing him- or herself and others. Despite this appeal, we risk seriously missing the underlying motivations for terrorism and significantly erring in the proper policy responses to reduce terrorism. Empirical research shows that the idea that terrorists are "crazy," or are suffering from a mental illness or a personality disorder, is simply not supported. Terrorists are not crazy. Beyond the mental illness hypothesis, several other researchers have attempted, with very limited success or empirical support, to explain and predict terrorism using well-established theories from psychology.

Research on the relationship between uncertainty and extremist behaviors, however, provides a more consistent account of why someone would be motivated to join a terrorist organization or to commit a terrorist act. Feelings of societal uncertainty motivate people to identify with social groups, which are best at reducing, controlling, or protecting against feelings of uncertainty. Terrorist organizations are particularly good at reducing uncertainty for potential members because they are highly entitative, or highly homogenous (all members think, feel, and behave the same way). When people identify with a highly entitative group, they feel more included; they strongly adhere to the group's norms, which makes them feel less uncertain. Simply put, terrorist groups are particularly well equipped to reduce this type of uncertainty. Preliminary evidence shows that uncertainty motivates people to identify with extremist groups, endorse extreme behaviors in the group, and take risks for the group. This perspective, while still needing more research, offers clearer, more defined prescriptions for counterterrorism, which we will discuss in more detail in Chapter 8.

## Notes

1. Callimachi and Porter 2018.
2. American Psychological Association (APA) 2013.

3. Crenshaw 1981; Jäger, Schmidtchen, and Süllwold 1981; Heskin 1984; Merari 1998.

4. Rasch 1979.

5. Post, Sprinzak, and Denny 2003.

6. Reich 1998; Silke 1998; Horgan 2003; Gill and Corner 2017.

7. Victoroff 2005.

8. Cooper 1977; Cooper 1978.

9. Pearce 1977.

10. J. Post 1998; J. Post 2004; Pedahzur, Perliger, and Weinburg 2003.

11. APA 2013.

12. Victoroff 2005.

13. Corner and Gill 2015; Gruenewald, Chermak, and Freilich 2013.

14. Ferracuti 1982; Ferracuti and Bruno 1981.

15. Ferracuti 1982.

16. Kaplan 1981.

17. J. Post 1998.

18. Strentz 1988.

19. Strentz 1988.

20. Merari et al. 2009.

21. Merari et al. 2009.

22. Krueger et al. 2008.

23. Bandura 1973.

24. Bandura, Ross, and Ross 1961.

25. Crenshaw 1992; Kelly and Rieber 1995; Atran 2003.

26. Crenshaw 1992; Kelly and Rieber 1995; Taylor and Quayle 1994.

27. Armstrong 2000; Marshall and Danizewski 2001.

28. Taylor and Quayle 1994.

29. Dollard et al. 1939; Friedland 1992.

30. Victoroff 2005.

31. Greenberg, Pyszczynski, and Solomon 1986; Greenberg, Solomon, and Pyszczynski 1997; Pyszczynski et al. 2004.

32. Friedman and Arndt 2005; Pyszczynski et al. 2004.

33. Dechesne et al. 2003; Friedman and Arndt 2005; Greenberg, Pyszczynski, and Solomon 1986.

34. Dechesne et al. 2003.

35. Arndt and Vess 2008; Burke, Martens, and Faucher 2010.

36. Pyszczynski et al. 2006.

37. Kruglanski et al. 2009; Kruglanski and Oreheek 2011; Kruglanski et al. 2014.

38. Dugas et al. 2016.

39. Zuckerman 1979.

40. Atran 2014; Hacker 1983; Levine 1999; Nussio 2017.

41. United Nations Security Council 2015.

42. Juergensmeyer 2000.

43. Schumpe et al. 2018.

44. Ekehammar et al. 2004; Henry et al. 2005.

45. Altemeyer 1998.

46. Pratto et al. 1994.

47. Ekehammar et al. 2004.

48. Lambert and Chasteen 1997.

49. Poteat and Mereish 2012.

50. Henry et al. 2005; Thomsen, Green, and Sidanius 2008.

51. Bryant et al. 1984.
52. Satterfield 1998.
53. Taylor and Quayle 1994.
54. Kruglanski and Fishman 2006.
55. Webster and Kruglanski 1994.
56. Cacioppo and Petty 1982.
57. Suedfeld, Tetlock, and Streudfert 1992.
58. Kruglanski and Fishman 2006.
59. Kruglanski and Fishman 2006; Victoroff 2005.
60. Henry et al. 2005.
61. Post, Sprinzak, and Denny 2003.
62. Post et al. 2016.
63. Gause 2014.
64. Hogg 2000, 2001, 2005.
65. Turner et al. 1987.
66. Campbell 1958; Hamilton and Sherman 1996.
67. Hogg 2005.
68. Hogg 2005.
69. Armstrong 2000.
70. Hohman and Hogg 2015.
71. Grieve and Hogg 1999; Hogg et al. 2007; Hogg, Meehan, and Farquharson 2010; Hohman and Hogg 2015; Hohman, Gaffney, and Hogg 2017.
72. Hogg, Meehan, and Farquharson 2010.
73. Hogg and Adelman 2013.
74. Goldman and Hogg 2016.
75. Hohman, Gaffney, and Hogg 2017.
76. Niedbala and Hohman 2019.
77. Niedbala et al. 2018.
78. Hofstede 1991; Stephan and Renfro 2002.
79. Kossowska and Sekerdej 2015; Sekerdej, Kossowska, and Czernatowicz-Kukeczka 2018.
80. Lind and van den Bos 2002.
81. McGregor 2006; McGregor and Marigold 2003; van den Bos et al. 2005.
82. McGregor et al. 2008.

6

# Myth: Terrorist Organizations Are Unsophisticated


TV action shows and nightly newscasts that terrorist organizations are loosely affiliated groups of ragtag mujahedeen, or "freedom fighters," living spartan lives in caves, like Osama bin Laden.[1] Terrorist "cells," as they are commonly called, conjure images of small groups of two to three people producing homemade bombs out of pressure cookers and cell phones. And, of late, "lone wolf" attacks, such as those in San Bernardino or Orlando, have stood out in the collective mind.[2] The problem is that this vision of a cellular or lone wolf structure also tends to support the incorrect assumption that terrorist groups are relatively unsophisticated and focus on targets of opportunity with no organizational goals or objectives. Like an amoeba, a terrorist organization moves somewhat randomly, consuming what it can, its growth limited by the size of its cells and its environment.

Further, this assumption paints a static view of terrorist organizations. They simply do not adapt (or do not need to because of their superior cellular/amorphous structure). Because these groups are so loosely affiliated, they are able to withstand external threats through the lack of connectivity, which isolates each group tactically and informationally (I cannot be compelled to give up my colleagues because I do not know who they are). These organizations are then perceived as impervious to external threats, obviating the need for new or adapted counterterrorism tactics. Coupled with assumptions about poverty, lunacy, and lack of education, current characterizations of terrorist organizations in the media and popular movies and television simply create an unrealistic view of how they are structured and operate, which leads to erroneous views about how to combat them.

## Upon Further Review

The chapter title suggests a question: Are terrorist organizations unsophisticated? In actuality, the mythical version of organizational structure presented above is a somewhat accurate description of some organizations, particularly at different times in their evolutionary development. But there is a plethora of organizational types, and terrorist organizations around the world run the gamut. As discussed below, organizational structures in terrorist organizations are not "one size fits all," and the differences, while seemingly subtle to casual observers, can have important implications for understanding organizations and planning how to combat them.

## Organizational Choice

It is tempting to view a terrorist organization's structure as a product of its external environment rather than as an active decision. Indeed, the external environment plays an important role, but terrorist organizations, like any group of individuals, face a complex choice involving scarce resources, personalities, goals, external factors, and so forth, and must evolve a structure (or change structures) based on those considerations. The "choice" of structure likely comprises a series of smaller choices made through time rather than the selection of a particular structure at the outset. The dynamic nature of these smaller choices, then, emphasizes how organizations change and adapt to changes in resources or the larger environment in which they operate. The following questions will help determine how an organization structures itself:

1. How does the organization link its goals and interests to the actions it can take to advance them?
2. How does it acquire and interpret information about the environment in which it operates?
3. How does it perceive its external audience, the constituencies that influence it, or those it hopes to influence?

4. What are the group dynamics and relationships among members (such as cohesion and internal conflicts)?
5. How do group preferences/tolerances for risk, deliberation of members before actions, or other factors influence the perceived costs/benefits of actions?

A few examples may help to clarify these questions. How does the way an organization links its goals and interests to its actions affect organizational choice? Consider the different objectives of the French Resistance and the American military during World War II. The former had limited resources and so could not take on German regular military formations. Therefore, it worked not to oust German troops but to disrupt their operations. The result was a loosely affiliated group of operators conducting smaller operations that was less susceptible to infiltration by spies and counterinsurgency operations. By contrast, the well-resourced US military undertook large movements and operations to remove the German army from France. As this objective required a larger resource base (men and material) and more logistical coordination, the resulting structure was quite different. D-day alone included 130,000 amphibious soldiers, 23,000 paratroopers, 1,500 tanks, 12,500 other vehicles, over 6,000 ships, and 10,000 aircraft.[3] That level of coordination requires a well-developed hierarchy of command and control with months of planning and practice.

Changes in goals and interests can also cause an organization to metamorphose through time. For example, ISIS began its life as a nascent Sunni-based insurgency against US and later Iraqi security forces. That objective and the resource base necessitated a very amorphous structure. But as ISIS grew into an attempted caliphate, it drew resources from a much broader geographical area[4] and required a major change in its organizational structure to one more suited to a bureaucratic state.

A second example is the evolution of al-Qaeda and the impact of internal conflicts and personalities. Prior to 2014, ISIS was, at least nominally, tied to the al-Qaeda network of terrorist organizations. In 2014, al-Qaeda formally disavowed ISIS due to its intransigence, its particularly brutal from of Salafism, and its open combat with the al-Qaeda-anointed Jabhat Al-Nusra in Syria.[5] This change likely happened in response to both the internal al-Qaeda conflict and perceptions of ISIS by external groups important to al-Qaeda for funding and political support. The federated relationship between ISIS and al-Qaeda could not survive the changes in ISIS tactics and objectives.

Finally, consider the role of leader risk aversion in organizational choice. For simplicity, only think about external threats. Both standard corporations and terrorist organizations face external threats, albeit from quite different sources. Take Microsoft or Google as examples. Both have faced significant competition in their fields, respectively operating systems and search engines. Both have prided themselves on their "decentralized" management.[6] But both companies have responded to the external threat of competition with greater levels of conglomeration, or accumulation of assets, power, and control through the acquisition of skill sets and assets from other companies.[7]

Al-Qaeda can loosely be thought of as a conglomeration as well, although, as we discuss later, there is perhaps a slightly better description of its organization. The primary difference in the strategy followed by al-Qaeda is that it comprises loosely affiliated organizations and does not have ownership control, like a corporation. In general, though, terrorist organizations face the external threat of detection and infiltration and even, to some extent, competition from other terrorist organizations. A risk-averse leader may be more prone to choose a loose cell structure to limit connectivity risk, but that choice necessarily limits the types of operations that can be mounted and the resources that can be brought to bear in operations. Thus, we may expect a more risk-averse leader to forgo some operational ability to avoid risk (more on risk in the next chapter).

Importantly, none of these factors operate in isolation. For example, a risk-averse leader may wish to minimize detection risk through decentralization, but external pressures and operational demands may require a more centralized system. We would predict here that, given the risk aversion, the organization will choose to minimize structural size as much as possible to successfully achieve its goals and minimize detection risk. And, of course, such choices are not always successful. Thus, the organization's ability to learn from its experiences and adapt impacts its success.[8] And that adaptation ability also makes combatting those groups more difficult. Just when we think we have an organization figured out, it morphs into something different.

The takeaway message here is that organizational structure is both dynamic and deliberative. Far from a random gang of ragtag warriors, terrorist groups are living organisms, and like more benign corporate organizations, they actively choose their structures in an evolutionary way, responding to external and internal requirements and pressures. Understanding them in this more dispassionate way will help to develop better predictive models of their future behavior. The next section further refines this view of terrorist organizations as producers.[9]

## The Terrorist Production Function

The "theory of the firm" in economics postulates that inputs are collected and utilized in some technical or relational way to generate outputs. In this sense, economics analyzes the what, who, and how questions relating to the production of goods and services. Terrorists can be viewed as the "unit of production" of terrorist violence.[10] That is, without the terrorist, there is no terrorism (this is the "supply side" of the market for terrorism mentioned in Chapter 2 and examined in more detail in Chapter 4).

Let's consider a simple corn-production example to frame the problem. A farmer has a given amount of resources available—land and labor, other inputs such as seed, water, and fertilizer, physical capital items like equipment, and technology such as GPS—to produce a crop. A technical relationship, called a production function, relates these inputs to output. For example, if you apply ten inches of water, you get a given yield, all else being equal; if you apply more water, you get more yield. In the absence of physical constraints such as a limited water supply, that function really involves no economics.

We must relate that production function to the costs of the inputs in order to generate a decision. In other words, if resources were free, we would simply use the amount needed to maximize the overall level of corn production. But resources are not free. So the farmer must relate the cost of each input applied to the value it produces.[11] Here the farmer is maximizing profit subject to physical constraints (such as water limitations) and input costs. Now, not all farmers are the same. A corn farmer in Iowa, for example, has a different set of technologies (think genetically modified seeds) and a different complement of resources (think labor availability) than a corn farmer in China. Thus the farmer in Iowa will organize his or her production (choose the optimal inputs and output) differently than the farmer in China, but both will maximize their profits subject to their individual constraints and prices. That is, an Iowa corn farm will likely be very capital intensive (lots of technology) with little labor compared to a low-tech, labor-intensive Chinese corn farm. Neither approach can be said to be "better" in the sense that both farms are doing the best they can, given their available resources, although the Iowa farm is almost certainly more efficient in terms of corn produced per amount of input. Further, external factors may change the decisions of the two farmers. Both face biological risk (say, from insect pressure). Access to the genetically modified seed that deters insects in Iowa will obviously result in a different decision to plant corn than in China and improve the productivity of the Iowa farm relative to the Chinese farm. Further, external effects such as the availability of crop insurance to protect against losses in Iowa will change that farmer's decision relative to the one in China even if all other resources and technologies are identical.

Terrorists likewise are simply attempting to optimize "profits" subject to resource constraints and costs. Profit, obviously, is loosely defined here as success in achieving desired objectives.[12] As for fertilizer, there is a market for suicide bombers in which supply and demand generate a "price."[13] There are similar markets for other skills/assets such as bomb makers, pilots, drivers, spiritual leaders, and so forth. The terrorist organization, then, must choose the combination of those inputs that maximize its success subject to the price/availability of those inputs. And each may have a different production function (resources and technology) that results in quite different choices in modes of production.

As in the US/Chinese farmer discussion, changes in production technology and resource availability will alter the "mix" of inputs used by terrorists. For example, after the US invasion of Afghanistan, al-Qaeda/Taliban insurgents adopted and widely used improvised explosive devices (IEDs) to attack US/NATO forces (as well as the local population). This adaptation in part arose out of the widespread availability of cellular phones and other electronic triggering devices as well as the need to conserve increasingly scarce human resources (unlike in a suicide bombing campaign). The success of this technology quickly spread to Iraq and other areas in a rapid technology diffusion driven by the relatively low cost of the technology and its ability to increase the production of lethality.[14] In another example, while the Israeli military was deployed in Lebanon during the early 1980s, Hezbollah utilized local cells to produce suicide attacks against military convoys and patrols. Once the Israeli military redeployed to a series of fortified posts in southern Lebanon (an area then known as the "Security Streep"), Hezbollah changed its tactics and started to use more conventional guerrilla tactics because suicide attacks against protected military posts have limited effectiveness.

The production function is both influenced by and influences the organizational structure of the "firm." In the farm example, a farm may be a sole proprietorship managed by a single manager or a complex corporation managed by many individuals (usually family members). Lower levels of technology are usually associated with higher production costs and smaller farm sizes that lend themselves to simple organizational structures. But advanced technology offers "economies of scale," which necessitate larger farms with more complex structures to minimize costs/maximize profits.

**Figure 6.1  Difference in Productivity of Labor with Differences in Technology**

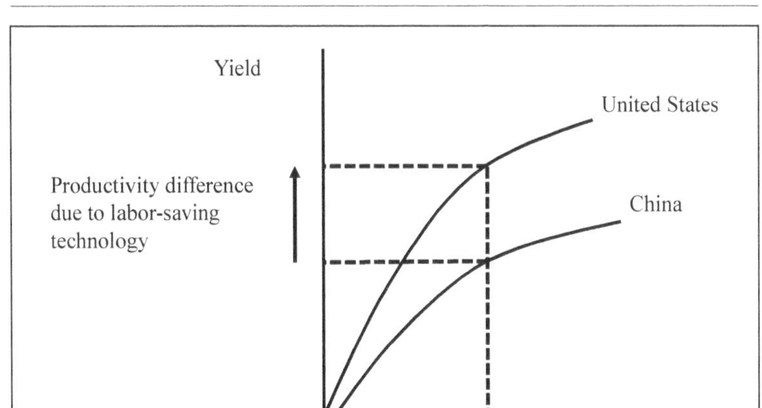


*Source:* Authors.

We can visualize the difference between countries/production systems by holding technology, for example, constant in each system and varying the amount of labor (see Figure 6.1). In both China and the United States, increasing labor increases output (at a generally decreasing rate). For any amount of labor, the United States produces more corn. The amount of technology in the United States versus China drives this productivity difference; that is, technology in this case enhances the productivity of labor, and because the United States has more technology, it gets more output per unit of labor input.

We can view terrorism through this lens. If we measure "yield" in casualties and are talking about knives and IEDs as technologies, we can see that the terrorist with the IED as opposed to the knife is likely to be more "productive." Thus, the ability of the terrorist organization to produce terror relates to the availability of labor (terrorists) as well as the technology that is brought to bear. Understanding these relationships can help us understand how terrorist organizations arrange their production (structure themselves) to maximize their goals.

Likewise, if resources are limited, and thus limit the terrorist group to small operations, a simple organizational structure will suffice. But the complexity of an operation like 9/11 would require a larger organization to manage the production process. Conversely, the size of the organization also influences the "productivity." For example, larger organizations are generally found to produce more lethal attacks.[15] Thus, the choice of organizational structure cannot be completely disentangled from the production technology and potential productivity, as those interact with one another in the choices made by the terrorist organization.

"Transaction cost" economics also offer some valuable insight into organizational structure.[16] In traditional corporations, the company must decide to "make or buy" products or inputs. For example, a car manufacturer must decide if it will make the radio for the car itself or contract with another company to do so. The decision hinges on the balance between the cost of owning the assets required to produce the radio (and the associated risks of ownership) and the costs of monitoring and enforcing contracts with other companies. That is, to make the radio itself, the car manufacturer must own the plant and equipment, hire the workers (and take on the associated employment costs), procure the inputs, optimize the plant for profitability, and so forth. But, at the same time, it maintains complete control over production (and quality) and can rest assured that the radios are produced how and when it wants. By contrast, if it contracts with a firm to produce them, it avoids the headaches of owning those assets and the costs associated with maintaining that infrastructure. So, Bose, for example, can produce radios for it and other car companies, thereby lowering the average cost of the radio for all. But the company becomes dependent on Bose for delivery of radios that meet its quality specifications when it needs them. This seemingly innocuous choice can be quite complex and depend on a lot of factors, such as leadership's risk aversion, legal constraints and costs, anticipation of future demand, and so forth.

Terrorist organizations face a similar, but in many cases more complex, decision. How do they produce terror? Do they "contract" bomb production or produce explosives in-house? Do they circumvent the potentially high costs of monitoring and enforcement (and detection) by maintaining a costly resource base of bomb makers or farm that out to other organizations? In most cases to date, terrorists have clearly valued the certainty of self-production over riskier "contractual" relationships to organize production. However, as we will see below, different types of network design facilitate resource sharing across organizations in some cases, thereby mimicking a "contractual" relationship for component delivery.

The upshot here is that terrorists produce terrorism, and the availability and "costs" of their inputs, their production technology, and their choice of organizational structure shapes how they do so. Next, we consider different types of organizations and networks to provide better insight into how terrorists organize themselves and the strengths and weaknesses of each type.

## Hierarchies, Networks, and "Dune" Organizational Hybrids

### Hierarchies

A terrorist group's organizational form, or the method by which it organizes command and control, communications, funding, and so forth, reflects its active choices. There are whole courses, books, and volumes of articles about organizational structure, and we will not go into those details here. There is considerable heterogeneity among specific organizational types, especially as they can morph. However, some generalizations about structure can yield a few insights.

Most readers are already, at least instinctively, familiar with hierarchical structures. We may be steeped in old war movies and accustomed to the idea of a commanding general and a chain of command that ends with the common grunt in the foxhole. Or we have seen organizational charts for companies that start at the CEO, then list subordinates organized by function or geography (or both). Perhaps hierarchies are encoded in our DNA given the long-standing social structures of monarchies and tribes.[17] Someone has to be in charge; someone has to be the worker bee.

Hierarchies have been around so long and been so successful because they do contain some real advantages over other organizational forms. For example, hierarchies (at least well-designed ones) have a clear chain of command. There is someone in charge to set goals and objectives and spread the work toward those goals across the organization. Now, those objectives could be developed through consensus or dictated (and that has implications for performance), but the structure moves messages up and down the chain and directs the efforts of the different members of the hierarchy. At the same time, the hierarchy promotes the division of labor, which allows the organization to benefit from economies of specialization (gaining more efficiency by limiting the scope of a task, such as having some employees go from making shoes to only making shoelaces).

Further, as the size of the organization grows, its functions generally become more complex, necessitating more sophisticated management. So, for example, a single baker may have one or two employees. The baker doesn't need much organizational structure because he basically directs all activities himself. But when the baker chooses to grow into a full-sized bakery that services local grocery stores, he now has a plant that operates twenty-four hours a day and employs many people, requiring an assistant manager, someone to procure inputs, an accountant, and so forth. As the bakery continues to grow, it opens multiple bakeries. Now the baker needs plant managers, a human resources manager, an attorney, and so on. The increase in business size is likely associated with declining average costs of production (economies of scale) but also means that organizational complexity increases as well. Hierarchical structures are usually employed to manage the sprawling bureaucracy necessary to manage such an enterprise. Especially relevant for terrorist groups is that hierarchical structures provide a clear line of succession as top leaders are frequently removed or killed through counterterrorism operations. The line of succession limits infighting and promotes organizational stability.

Growing structural size, while generally associated with improved operational efficiencies, is not without pitfalls. We generally classify these problems in a class of behavior called the principal-agent problem.[18] Because the management (the upper part of the hierarchy or the principal) becomes increasingly detached from the workers (the agents), ensuring that agents expend the maximum effort to achieve organizational goals becomes increasingly difficult. As an extreme example, the CEO of AT&T has no idea how much time the janitor at the Hyderabad, India, call center spends hiding in the broom closet each day to avoid work. Workers' choices influence the performance of the organization, but the principals can only imperfectly (and at a certain expense) monitor those choices. Generally, the greater the "distance" between the principal and the agent, the higher the cost of monitoring and/or loss of productivity. This is not to say that distance "guarantees" bad performance. But distance certainly increases the incentive/opportunity for the agent to shirk work and increases the cost of monitoring to ensure shirking does not happen.

Terrorist organizations are not dissimilar to businesses in this regard, but with subtle and not-so-subtle differences in the problems and remedies. When, like the baker, terrorist organizations are quite small, they have little need for organizational design. But as the size of their organization grows, they encounter similar needs to coordinate activities, minimize costs, capture economies of specialization and scale, and so forth. And terrorist organizations ultimately face principal-agent problems, as demonstrated by the rupture between ISIS and al-Qaeda, when al-Qaeda (the principal) was no longer able to exert control over ISIS (the agent).[19]

But terrorist organizations also face the complicating factor that they must minimize the risk of detection of their illicit activities. This risk compounds the potential principal-agent problems found in traditional organizations. To succeed, terrorists need to have competent and loyal workers. A sprawling organization faces the risk of recruiting workers that will "rat" or shirk their responsibilities, with potentially devastating results. Herein lies the key weakness of hierarchies for terrorists as compared to companies. For a company, shirking likely leads to slightly higher costs of production (through lower labor productivity). For a terrorist, shirking could cause the downfall of the organization.[20]

Again, ISIS provides a useful example. In its nascent state, ISIS maintained its more classical amorphous organization of loosely affiliated groups executing smaller operations of disruption against US and Iraqi forces (and rebel groups in Syria). As it grew in size and territorial control, however, the demands of administering a "state" required a more precise division of labor and command and control that led to a more traditional hierarchy. As we might expect, this metamorphosis resulted in greater efficiency of administration.[21] We even have records and receipts from ISIS-held territories as evidence of the extent of the organization's administrative development. At the same time, that increased efficiency exposed ISIS to greater degrees of the principal-agent problem and potentially created more opportunities for infiltration, monitoring, and attack by counterterrorism forces.

The weaknesses of traditional hierarchies are not unknown to terrorists. And while we generally expect terrorist organizations to become more hierarchical as they grow, traditional hierarchies simply describe their structures less effectively than we would like. For a more realistic view, then, we turn to social networks as a better model.

## Networks

Networks provide a useful way to visualize the interconnectedness of terrorist organizations, which can help predict things such as information flow, command and control, recruitment, and so forth. Figures 6.2, 6.3, and 6.6 illustrate three broad types of networks: chain, hub or star, and multi. The connector lines in each show the paths of potential communication to show the connectivity between nodes. Different strengths and weaknesses characterize each of these types in different environments. As previously mentioned, there is much heterogeneity within each type, although these three general structures assist with understanding major structural differences.

In the chain network (Figure 6.2), considered optimal for smuggling or trafficking operations, communication is sequential. It may be bidirectional between specific nodes, but one end of the chain does not speak with the other end. We might compare this to more traditional project management in which a sequence of events takes place, and while changes or modifications may occur between steps, the overall plan is established, then financed, and then operationalized. Command and control is pretty flexible and largely consists of sets of instructions; there is little direction from external entities. The advantage here is that the operation is compartmentalized and so less susceptible to detection, but its reliance on each node executing the project with little external control can lead to potential breakdowns when one node is compromised or removed.

A hub or star network (Figure 6.3), by contrast, is characterized by strict central control of relatively unconnected nodes of operation. The "cells" are linked only through the center, so failure of one node has little impact on other nodes (unlike in the chain), and detection of one node is simply handled by cutting its ties to the center. Readers most likely visualize the star network when they think of terrorist "cells" and "networks." However, this type is used mostly with sleeper cells (the USS *Cole* bombing), when the "mother" organization constructs the cell to reduce external infiltration and detection. In homegrown cells not monitored by external experienced operators, we will often see something close to an "all-channel" network, in which all members are highly connected to each other (the 7/7 bombing in London), mainly because of the

## Figure 6.2   Visualization of a Chain Network

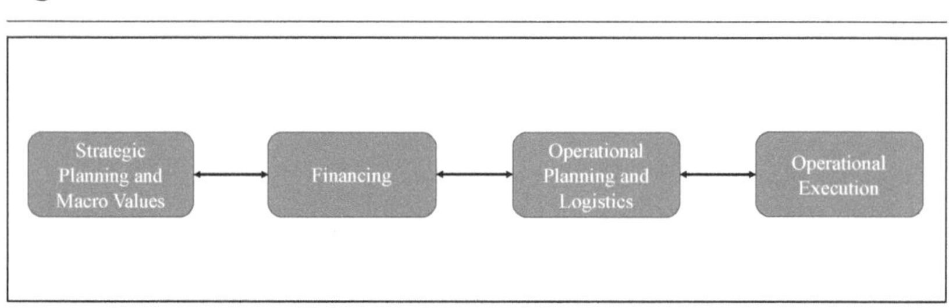


*Source:* Authors, adapted from discussion in Mishal and Rosenthal 2005.

## Figure 6.3    Visualization of a Hub or Star Network

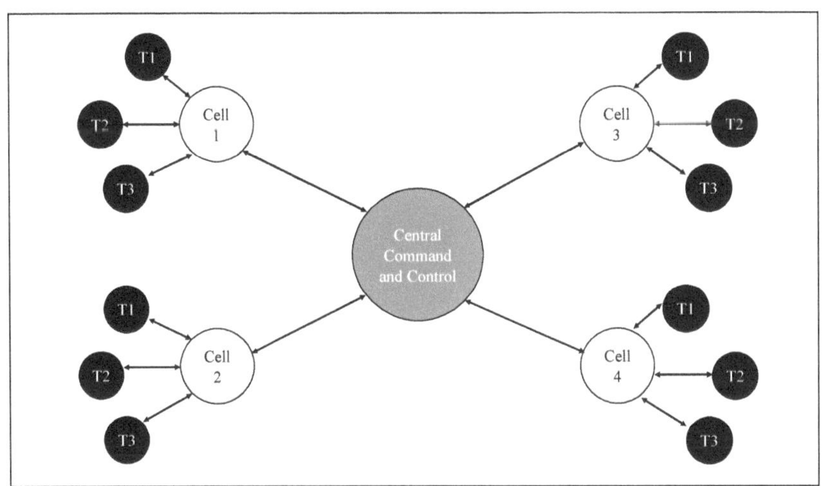


*Source:* Authors, adapted from discussion in Mishal and Rosenthal 2005.

network's spontaneous growth and the common limited operational experience of its members. Figure 6.4 illustrates the network associated with the USS *Cole* bombing. Note that a few well-connected nodes provide command and control and are likely linked to the mother organization. However, most members are not well connected to enable easy severing of ties in case of detection.

By contrast, Figure 6.5 depicts the 7/7 London bombing's homegrown network. Note that each member is highly connected with the entire network. Because these networks arise spontaneously, they result in members who are highly familiar with each other. Naturally, star networks are more vulnerable to direct targeting of the hub (decapitation of the leader), while homegrown cells are more vulnerable to infiltration, because of the high level of familiarity of even marginal actors with the entire network.

Finally, the multinetwork (Figure 6.6) includes multiple subgroups connected via several hubs (usually termed a "scale-free" network). It has no defined "center" of control, and command is more flexible and diffuse. Multiple lines of communication between nodes allow two or more nodes to communicate and coordinate activities. This structure allows more economies of specialization to increase efficiency (lower costs) so that, for example, a node specializing in

**Figure 6.4   Social Network of Terrorists in the Bombing of the USS *Cole* (suicide bombers depicted by largest circles)**

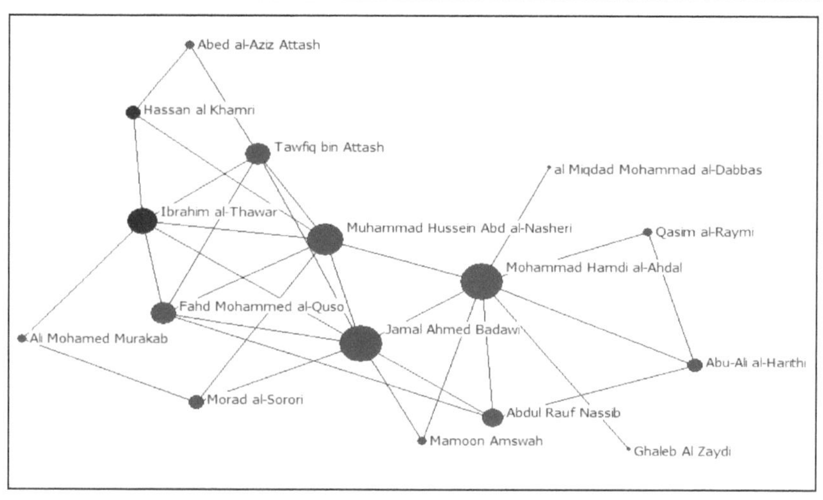


*Source:* Authors.

transportation can coordinate with a node with a comparative advantage in financing in order to move materials around to more efficiently conduct operations. However, the increased interconnectivity increases the risk of detection/infiltration and makes ensuring quality of production across the network more difficult.

Older, more established, or more administrative terrorist groups such as Hezbollah and ISIS have developed fairly well-defined hierarchical structures with vertical communication lines and rigid frameworks for division of labor and chain of command.[22] Hamas, conversely, used both star and homegrown networks as it built its base against Israel in the 1980s. However, it used chain networks to compartmentalize operations between military and social functions, hoping to use its social functions as a shield against public criticism. But it also used a hub network to connect the compartmentalized operations through a very strict central control. Finally, groups such as the Palestinian Islamic Jihad used multinetworks to connect with other radical Islamic terrorist groups such as the Fatah movement. These loose connections allowed groups to specialize and to share information and assets with other groups.[23]

**Figure 6.5    Social Network of the 7/7 London Bombing (suicide bombers depicted by largest circles)**

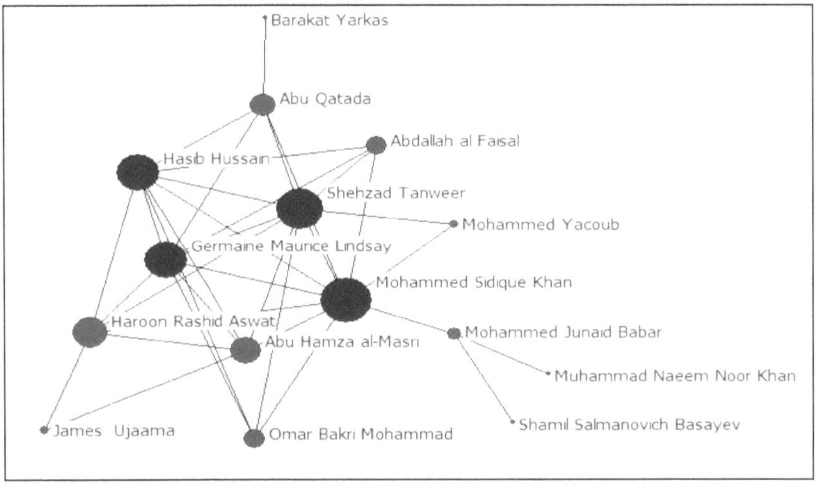

*Source:* Authors.

Notwithstanding the particular structure, understanding social networks can help with understanding terrorist organizations and operations. Network analysis has been instrumental in coming to grips with major social issues such as disease spread and internet operations. In the classic model of epidemiology (disease spread), you can interact with another person who carries a disease (say, influenza), with some probability that once exposed, you will contract the flu. If you do, you then expose others with whom you interact, who have a probability of contracting the flu, and so on. In this classic network, the probability of infection matters more than the "connectivity." Your not contracting the flu this time has little impact on your probability of contracting it in a subsequent interaction (presuming you are not naturally immune, in which case your probability of infection is always zero).

Social networks, however, are different. The strength of association matters. That is, how well you know a friend likely impacts how much weight you put on information he or she provides you (we will return to this concept in Chapter 7 in more detail). This distinguishing feature of social networks makes them a very rich way to understand organizational outcomes. For example, research has shown that in a network analysis of Palestinian suicide attacks, factors such as the strength of

## Figure 6.6   Visualization of a Multinetwork

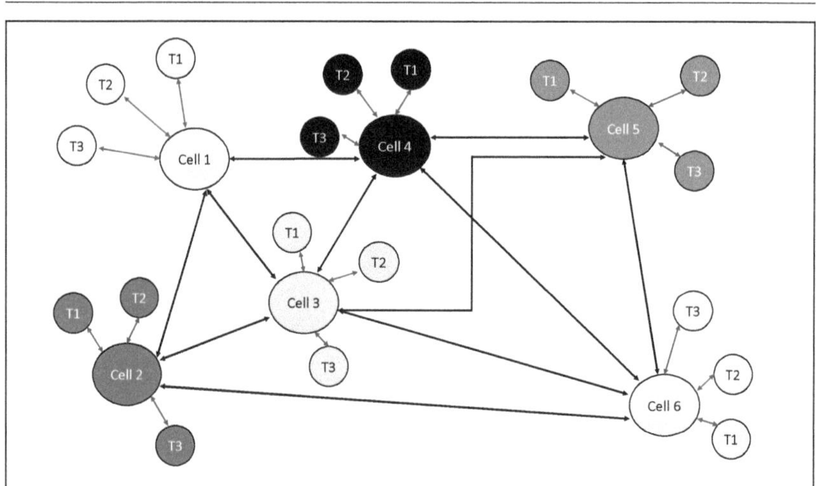


*Source:* Authors, adapted from discussion in Mishal and Rosenthal 2005.

association of bombers with central planning hubs impacts effectiveness, and the peripheral network of suicide bomber "clusters" is a better explanatory variable for suicide attacks than the organizational structure of the larger terrorist organization itself.[24] The use of social network analysis provides great opportunities for furthering our understanding of terrorist organizations and how to combat them.[25]

## Of Amoebas and Sand Dunes

The title of this chapter poses a question about the organizational structure of terrorist organizations. Like an online relationship status—it's complicated. Further complicating our understanding of organizational structure is the fact that structure is not rigid and fixed; rather, it is evolutionary. ISIS evolved from an amorphous conglomeration of radical Salafist Sunni groups conducting an insurgency into a highly administrative "state" of quite developed bureaucratic hierarchies.

Other organizations, such as al-Qaeda, are more difficult to pigeonhole, in part because their structures seem to "shift with the wind," like sand. Some researchers have taken to calling these "dune" organizations.[26] As the wind pours across a desert, the sands move and shift, taking the path of least resistance, forming new dunes and consuming (and then re-exposing) ground as it moves around. A sand dune is obviously there. We see it. But it has no defined structure. It simply is—and then is not—in front of our eyes as the winds change.

The analogy to a sand dune is instructive. As the political or economic winds change, al-Qaeda simply morphs and changes with them. It carries some of the characteristics of hierarchies—bin Laden as a leader with key lieutenants responsible for different functions—as well as hub and multinetworks. A defining characteristic is that al-Qaeda operates globally and across different types of domains (suicide bombings, direct attacks on government assets, education, etc.), but it is often not the sole, or even the primary, source of the terrorist activity in an area. Rather, as al-Qaeda takes on a new role or morphs across geography, it either forms alliances with existing groups or develops nascent terrorist groups to meet its objectives. As it either accomplishes its objective in an area or feels comfortable that its new affiliate can stand on its own with its own resources, it moves on. So, like a sand dune, it shifts around without a clearly defined structure or clearly observable center, making tracking and attacking it incredibly difficult.[27]

## Concluding Remarks

The popular perception that terrorist groups are simply loose associations of cells with no real conscious organizational structure, while sometimes descriptive, is simply too narrow to fully explain how or why terrorists organize themselves the way they do. Research into these groups makes clear that they do, in fact, make rational strategic choices about their internal organization.

Some of the rationale for those organizational choices bears a striking resemblance to why companies organize in particular ways: providing efficiency and division of labor, facilitating and protecting communication flows, organizing production units to reach maximum profit, and so forth. Clearly, both companies and terrorist groups are responding to their external environments in terms of resource availability, prices, competition, and the like. But terrorist organizations clearly also face different pressures, such as detection and infiltration, which may cause them to forgo some of the efficiencies gained through a more defined structure.

The key message here is that we cannot simply assume that terrorist organizations will organize their operations as cell networks only, and their structures may differ vastly depending on the environments in which they operate. It is safe to assume that any structure we observe today may morph dramatically (and rapidly) in response both to changes in external conditions or internal objectives and to pressures we place on them through counterterrorist activities. In this regard, attention to how/why structures form is critical in predicting responses and finding weaknesses to exploit.

## Notes

1. Hirschkorn and Bergen 2015.
2. Worth 2016.
3. Raworth, n.d.
4. Dodwell, Milton, and Rassler 2016.
5. Sly 2014.
6. See, for example, Wharton School of Business (2013) relating to Microsoft's reorganization from a decentralized management to a centralized system, especially with regard to technology-development decisions.
7. Sherman 2008.
8. Jackson 2009.
9. Readers are directed to Shapiro (2013) for a comprehensive examination of managing terrorist organizations.
10. Jackson 2009.
11. In purely technical terms, we are relating the value of the additional corn produced for each additional input applied to the cost of that additional input.
12. Like any organization, terrorist organizations generally have short-term goals such as maximizing the number of successful attacks and long-term goals such as defeating the government. And like any ordinary organization, they must consider short- and long-term decisions simultaneously.
13. Iannaccone 2006.
14. Interestingly, according to Singer (2012), IEDs have a long history but enjoyed little strategic importance until the more recent conflicts in Afghanistan, Iraq, and Syria.
15. Asal and Rethemeyer 2008.
16. Williamson 1979.
17. Haidt 2013.
18. Milgram and Roberts 1992.
19. Sly 2014.
20. Readers are referred to Berman and Laitin (2008) for a good discussion of defection constraints in terrorist organizations to reduce defection and shirking.
21. Callimachi 2018; Dodwell, Milton, and Rassler 2016.
22. Mishal and Rosenthal 2005.
23. Mishal and Rosenthal 2005.
24. Pedahzur and Perliger 2006.
25. Ressler 2006.
26. Mishal and Rosenthal 2005.
27. The amoeba also serves as a metaphor for this behavior as well, except that the amoeba has a clear cellular center, and while it does move about rather amorphously, once it consumes a neighbor, it tends not to let that neighbor go and simply grows in size.

# 7

# The Influence of the
# Media and Governments

*Make no mistake: we face a deadlier threat than ever before not only because our enemies have gotten savvier, but because we took the pressure off them.*
    —House Homeland Security Chairman Michael McCaul (R-TX)[1]

What is the probability of one's having a heart attack? Most people probably do not know the answer to questions like this and so rely on perceptions of the riskiness or probability of an event occurring to make decisions. Consider, for example, Chapman University's *Study of American Fears* in 2016, which reported that 38.5 percent of survey respondents feared being the victim of a terrorist attack—slightly more than feared being the victim of identity theft.[2] This mirrors an earlier study finding that 30.8 percent of Americans were "very concerned" about themselves or a friend or relative being a victim of a terrorist attack.[3] Thus, the perceived risk of falling victim to terrorism is not only high but persistently high. This chapter uses the lens of how people perceive risk to explore how terrorists influence the public, shape people's actions and decisions, and use information (communication) and, ultimately, how the public's own communication can be used against them. Along the way, however, we are going to challenge some common preconceived notions in the public's reactions to terrorism and how those reactions are being used against it by both the government and terrorists.

## Upon Further Review: Risk, Risk Aversion, and the True Power of Terrorism

People live in an uncertain world, and this uncertainty impacts the decisions they make every day, from long-term retirement planning to what types of foods to eat. We are inundated with information about these issues constantly, and some of the information only adds to the uncertainty. "Salt is bad for you." "Well, maybe it's not." Regardless of the uncertainty, decisions about actions must be made. Technically, we are referring to risk. At the most basic level, two related variables—risk and risk tolerance—influence decisions under uncertainty. "Risk" is the objective (actual) probability that an event will occur. For example, what is the probability of being involved in a terrorist incident this year? From 2002 through 2015, roughly 346 casualties (deaths and injuries) resulted from known terrorist acts in the United States.[4] This means that an individual's probability of being involved in a terrorist incident in the United States over that period was 0.000012 percent—a very, very small number. A person is literally more likely to be crushed by falling furniture than killed by a terrorist.[5]

Given the stark and obvious difference between the raw probability and our perception of an event occurring, Americans (and others) grossly overestimate the risk. But our inability to accurately assess risk is not limited to terrorism. For example, Americans (both smokers and nonsmokers) substantially overestimate the risk of lung cancer from smoking.[6] Early research even indicated that exposure to news of an adverse event affected people's perceived risks of unrelated events.[7] Even our personality type is likely to affect how we perceive risk.[8]

Our perception of risk profoundly shapes how we react to potential situations, but risk tolerance, called the level of risk aversion (see the appendix to this chapter for a more technical explanation), also influences decisions. Generally, we classify people into one of three categories. "Risk-neutral" people do not really consider risk in their decisions. Their primary concern is the expected return or outcome of an event. By far the largest group in the population includes the "risk-averse." These people prefer less risk to more and are willing to give up some amount of income or benefit (called a risk premium) to shift risk to someone else or to be compensated if the event occurs. Finally, "risk seekers" are adrenaline junkies. They seek out risk. Their idea of fun is cliff diving or a late night at the blackjack table. Of course, there are gradations of both risk seeking and risk aversion. For example, a highly risk-averse person likely has a thirty-two-character password of random numbers and letters on his computer, whereas a slightly risk-averse person probably uses a combination of her kids' birthdays. The highly risk-averse person is trading ease of memory for security. The slightly risk-averse person is willing to take more risk of being hacked in favor of remembering her password without perpetually having to hit the "forgot password" link on her bank's website.

As most people are risk-averse to some degree, we expect them to pursue actions that reduce their risks. For example, risk-averse individuals will purchase property insurance regardless of whether they are required to do so by law or the bank. They will purchase security systems for their homes. They will not walk through unlit parking lots alone. Or they will cancel vacations for fear of a terrorist attack. Some might call these actions "prudent." But the degree of "prudence" matters. Even on a broader scale, risk-averse individuals will gladly forgo some civil liberties in the name of reducing terrorist risk and/or demand more government spending on antiterrorist activities. The key here is that risk-averse individuals will forgo something of value to reduce the probability that an event will happen to them (or to be compensated if that event occurs).

The combination of our perceived risks and our risk aversion drives our decisions. For any level of risk aversion, as our perceived risks rise, our willingness to forgo things of value to avoid those risks rises as well. Likewise, for any level of perceived risk, if our risk aversion rises, we will forgo more things of value as well. Disaggregating decisions in this manner helps explain why we observe behavior in a particular way, even if people's choices seem irrational on the surface. So, for example, it may be perfectly rational for someone to refuse to play blackjack at a casino but to go skydiving on the weekend. In the former instance, they simply view the risk of loss as quite high; in the latter, they feel safe because of the reliability of the safety equipment. It matters little whether they are correctly assessing the risk in each scenario because perceived risks matter in decisionmaking.[9] And the fact that perceived risk matters (combined with a lack of understanding of true probabilities) opens decisions to influence by outside forces and information. This is especially relevant for understanding government's response to terrorism. As discussed further in this and the next chapter, studies show that the policymakers' threat (risk) perception with regard to terrorism is the single most important element that determines which counterterrorism measure will be implemented.

## Perceived Threats Versus Anxiety

We live in a dynamic world, and perceptions about potential risks are not constant. How we react to an event taking place shapes future actions and creates opportunities/avenues through which terrorists and governments, friends and organizations influence perceptions. Consider the dichotomous description of a potential reaction to terrorism in Figure 7.1.

### Perceived Threats

When a terrorist event occurs (or the potential for an event is recognized), we can view the event as an external threat to well-being. When people feel threatened by the existence of terrorism/terrorists, they usually react with anger, and that anger is usually associated with a desire to reject nongroup members (often expressed as xenophobia), particularly immi-

**Figure 7.1    The Differential Effects of Perceived Threats vs. Anxiety on Our Reactions to Terrorism**

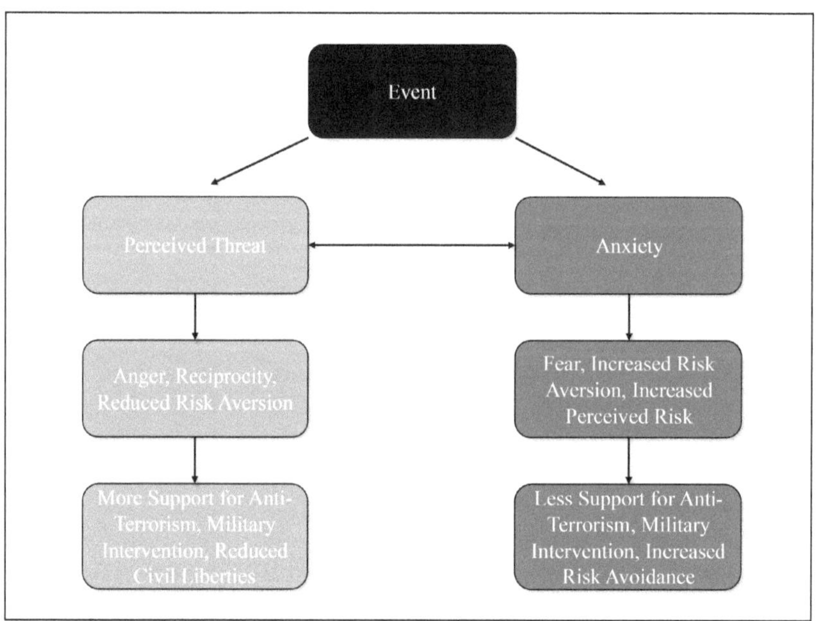


*Source:* Authors, visualization adapted from the verbal description in Huddy et al. 2005.

grants and ethnic minorities (recall the discussion about perceived threats and responses in Chapter 5).[10] Further, among political leaders, perceived external threats and the anger they generate lead to more dogmatic decisionmaking and an almost self-reinforcing negative view of the enemy or source of the threat.[11] In what may seem obvious only after the fact, feeling threatened tends to increase aggregate support for political candidates/leaders viewed as powerful and active.[12] Overall, then, anger and desire for reciprocity reduce our level of risk aversion.[13]

Because risk aversion lies at the core of decisionmaking, that reduction in aversion leads to changes in willingness to act. Particularly, lower risk aversion equates to a willingness to engage in riskier actions such as direct military intervention[14] or increased antiterrorism activities. People wish to inflict greater damage on the enemy (an in-group benefit) even if that brings a higher risk of negative consequences (deaths or other in-group harms). The prototypical Facebook "troll" reader is thinking, "Of course those idiots are willing to send other people's sons and daughters to their deaths—no cost to them." Despite its being easier to "play with other people's money," we prefer to presume that people are reacting psychologically to a perceived threat—having a fight or flight autonomic response—rather than to ascribe some other (usually unsubstantiated) motivation. It should be noted that politicians are risk-averse as well,[15] and the political implications of not taking action could be loss in the next election, and so they are more willing to take action to avoid the appearance of "doing nothing."

Finally, feeling threatened by terrorist activities often leads to the undermining of civil liberties. For example, about 56 percent of Americans favored implementation of national identification cards in the aftermath of 9/11, with a smaller number (31 percent) favoring government monitoring of citizen communications.[16] Critics often react emotionally to this response as xenophobic, "un-American," or irrational. However, viewed dispassionately, this is simply a logical response to perceived threats when viewed through the lens of risk aversion. If we treat civil liberties (and the benefits that flow from them) as "expected returns," the willingness to give up some expected returns to reduce the perceived risks is precisely what the theory of risk aversion would predict. Now, we can certainly debate whether that risk premium in the form of foregone civil liberties reduces risk or whether we are overestimating the risk in the first place, but to presume the response is irrational on its face does little to further the debate about true costs and benefits.

The problem here is not that people are risk-averse or even that we often misunderstand the actual risk of terrorism (both interesting issues worthy of investigation). Rather, the problem in this context arises when government, media, and other information sources manipulate our natural reaction to risk to their benefit. Consider the quote at the beginning of this chapter. Representative Michael McCaul's statement at the beginning of this chapter hits the key elements in our model of reaction. First, it identifies the terrorists as "threats." Next, it infers that the threat has increased precisely because we have reduced action against those threats. We do not wish to overascribe motives here, but such framing of statements is specifically designed to evoke action rather than passivity. Readers who perceive terrorism as a threat likely agree with this statement, and that is natural. But our natural reaction to perceived threats can be used to galvanize support for a riskier course of action to the benefit of those who receive funding, jobs, and so forth, as a result of the public's demand for action. And note that this sort of manipulation is not limited to terrorism. The issues of climate change, illegal drugs, and illegal immigrants are framed in this manner to galvanize action. Not everyone buys the threat arguments, of course, creating "skeptics." But wording matters, and this approach has proven relatively successful time and again.

## Anxiety

Instead of anger, an actual or potential terrorist event can generate anxiety, which induces fear, with the associated increases in risk aversion and/or perceived risk. Higher levels of anxiety typically correlate with less support for antiterrorism activities or military intervention[17] and likely lead to actions that increase risk avoidance. Think of those who will not travel abroad for fear of terrorism or "preppers" and "off-the-grid" proponents who stock up on ammunition and food in case of an attack. Again, if you view the world through the "threat" lens, you are likely shaking your head at the absurdity of this reaction. But, again, based on the psychological response of anxiety, these actions are perfectly rational. If an event leads to a perception of higher risk or makes one less tolerant of risk, then the associated responses flow naturally from these changes.

But just as governments might manipulate threat perceptions to generate a more robust, less risk-averse response from the public, terrorists play into feelings of anxiety to manipulate behavior as well. In fact, this is, in large part, the goal of terrorism in the first place. Terrorists want to increase anxiety levels so that a populace will "crawl into its shell" and demand "appeasement" of their wishes.[18] Of course, anxiety manifests in our reactions in different ways. Some may rationalize their anxiety through pseudo-intellectual arguments such as "Well, our foreign policies *do* oppress their people, and so they are just defending themselves." Or the more direct "If we escalate our response, they will simply increase the number and intensity of attacks against us." But the upshot of these reactions is that we prefer to defuse the perceived risk rather than confront it or continue to be exposed to it.

Like those of the "threat" crowd, the "anxiety" crowd's responses project from their core reaction to an event or the prospect of an event. We provide no moral judgment as to the "correctness" of one reaction over the other. Rather, the key is to understand how our reactions are derived, their implications, and how they can be used against us or manipulated to achieve the desired outcomes of others. Further, if we understand how our friends, neighbors, and, yes, even our social media "enemies" are forming their reactions, we can then begin to develop a more rational, less emotional response to the potential for future terrorist events.

## Managing Information and Playing Above Your Capability

### The Media and Terrorism

Whether the media like to admit it or not, media and terrorism have a symbiotic relationship.[19] This mutual benefit can be quite indirect, as is the case with Western media, or it can amount to overt collusion, as in some parts of the world with significant terrorist influence. Terrorism sells, and terrorists need cheap advertising. People are interested in information about terrorism. They want to be informed about events around the world and at home, and the media seek that information out and (these days) deliver it directly to our desktops. Terrorists do not possess massive media conglomerates and advertising agencies, although groups such as ISIS became quite adept at utilizing low-cost digital media for effect.[20] Thus, terrorists rely on mass/social media to deliver their messages to broad audiences.

These underlying motivations generate a symbiotic relationship, which can become quite self-reinforcing.[21] That is, the desire to gain media coverage provides incentives for terrorists to invest in perpetrating highly "dramatic" attacks, and the subsequent reporting of such attacks can further incentivize terrorists to seek more innovative and "dramatic" tactics. This concept likely led to then secretary of state

John Kerry to quip in a speech in Bangladesh, "Perhaps the media would do us all a service if they didn't cover it quite as much. People wouldn't know what's going on."[22] Of course, though not very nuanced (and taken out of context from a much longer speech), this statement was not completely irrational given what we know about the media and information.

## Information Cascades

The term *information cascade* refers to a phenomenon in social networks where a piece of information enters a network and begins to influence its members, often exponentially. Because we most often lack complete knowledge about an issue or topic, we rely on outside information to make judgments. A simple example will help illustrate. A new bistro has opened in the area, which people know little about. Consider some sources of information. First, an acquaintance tells you that it is quite good. OK, but you really do not know this person's taste in food. Second, the local newspaper reviews the bistro and calls it "mediocre." Finally, your best friend calls and says the place is great! You have two pieces of information from people you know and one piece from a third party with a reputation for picking good restaurants. What do you do?

The example points to two differential effects: strength of connection and quantity of reinforcing information. Most will likely try the place because they know their friend's tastes (assuming they like the same foods) and have another piece of reinforcing information. The third piece of information conflicts but is overpowered by the strength of connection with friends and the reinforcing information. The cumulative effect of reinforcing information and connection strength is called a cascade.

More broadly, we are exposed to information about events. Evidence shows that people are most likely to weigh information from sources more heavily when they share the same values or are perceived to be "in the same boat."[23] Think of it this way. Does one tend to believe a politician who says we need to go to war more when his or her son or daughter's combat unit is being deployed? People probably give the opinion more weight even when they disagree. But in addition to the "strength of connection" element, there is also the sheer volume of information. The more often we hear the same fact from different sources, the more we come to believe it to be true regardless of its validity. So, while "repeating a lie often enough does not make it true," doing so probably increases the likelihood it will be believed.

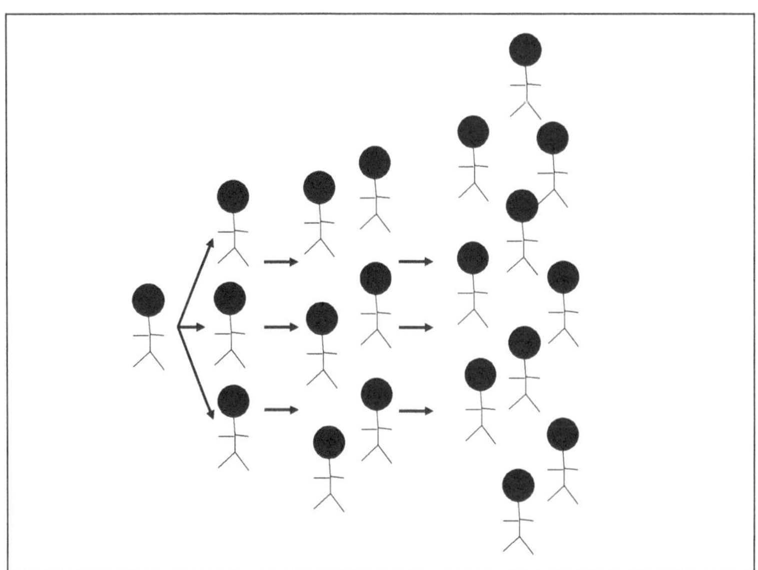

Figure 7.2   An Information Cascade

*Source:* Authors.

The 2000 movie *Pay It Forward* is loosely based on the concept of an information cascade (Figure 7.2). Assume that you share a piece of information with three close friends. Assume further that those three friends share that information with three of their close friends. At that moment, your piece of information has reached twelve people (your three plus each of their three). Assuming our rule of threes continues, you can see that the information is spreading exponentially. So, your message is "going viral." The concept of the exponential spread of information is central to social networks and information cascades. Of course, the speed of information flow can be "good" or "bad" in nature. Mark Twain purportedly once said (most likely paraphrasing something Jonathan Swift wrote in 1710), "A lie can travel halfway around the world while the truth puts its pants on." Internet rumors, false quotes, bad memes, and any other number of items have been used to spread false information quickly and effectively.

Given the potential multiplication effect of information cascades, now go back and consider Figure 7.1 again. Both governments and terrorists want to influence perceptions about events or the potential for events, and both use the media to do it. On the one hand, governments may use the media to stress the "threat" nature of terrorism, focus on actions being taken to prevent it, and highlight the impacts or risks of not actively addressing it. They are, of course, attempting to galvanize support for counterterrorism. Terrorists, on the other hand, attempt to use media to display their exploits and publicize their activities to cultivate anxiety within their target population. They focus on the horrific results of opposing them and on intimidating populations into acquiescence to their operations.

Framing matters a lot.[24] The presentation of these stories will help shape reactions. But also important is the strength of our connections with the media or a particular media source and the people with whom we associate and discuss these issues (information cascades). We know that media will slant their coverage to fit the preconceptions of their target audiences,[25] and so viewers/readers receive a cascade of self-reinforcing views that seem to confirm their unconscious biases. While the media have the capacity to vastly influence outcomes through these information cascades, far from being in control, they appear to be pawns in the game of informational chess between governments and terrorists. Further, our own cultural, political, and economic self-segregation has led to ever more isolated "bubbles" vulnerable to the type of self-reinforcing information cascades discussed here.[26] Ultimately, then, it is no wonder that different groups have such strongly held beliefs and reactions, be they "threat" or "anxiety" based. For most Americans, they hear nothing else all day long from their media sources and friends, which leads to the depersonalization of members outside your "group," as discussed in Chapter 5.

## Media and Terrorist Strategies

There are very significant similarities between the media strategies of terrorists and those of other types of activist groups. There are many theories about and descriptions of individual tactics used, but the overarching strategy is to find a balance between action and the threat of action that achieves desired results at minimum cost or expenditure of resources. Basically, we are talking about reputation.

A classic example from the nonterrorist world is that of the organization People for the Ethical Treatment of Animals (PETA). While it claims to have over 3 million members, PETA only employs around three hundred staff; yet it challenges some of the largest companies in the world. PETA's strategy focuses on two primary areas. First, it uses graphic "shock" ads to garner attention in the noisy world of advertising.[27] The purpose is to create a revulsion for meat consumption or other activities related to meat production and processing.[28] PETA is attempting to stir up a "threat" response that galvanizes action against the meat-production sector.

But advertising alone is insufficient. "The boy who cried wolf" syndrome will quickly overtake your efforts and leave you viewed as "all talk and no action." To be taken seriously, the activist must have some reputation for effectively inflicting damage (physical or economic) on the target. Essentially, activists are playing a game with companies or governments in which there is uncertainty about whether (1) the activist is willing to actually engage in an activity that will inflict damage and (2) whether the activist is able to inflict damage.[29] The stronger the reputation for action (or effectiveness when action is taken), the more likely the activist is to generate a desired response. Thus, the more media coverage one can generate, the more effective activities seem and the more "cred" the organization gets. Thus, using shock advertising and widely promoting small but effective protests makes an organization appear larger and more effective than it otherwise might.[30]

Terrorists take this strategy to the extreme. Photos and videos of ISIS beheading innocent civilians and soldiers have tremendous "shock value." The organization is both literally and symbolically beheading its enemies.[31] Despite the symbolism, however, the intent is clear. ISIS means business and is letting everyone know about it. Again, the multiplier effect of media comes into play in this strategy. The use of shocking videos or photographs leads news agencies to run the story continuously for a time, and the repetitive nature of the story makes it seem as though it happens more frequently, giving the terrorist instant credibility. And, true to the theory, once that credibility is established, the mere threat alone can cause diversion of resources to prevent the action and raise anxiety levels. So, for example, a bomb threat (by either a terrorist group or an attention seeker) results in an immediate large response, diverting precious resources from other areas.

The brilliance of the strategy is its brutal simplicity. Antiterror pundits often comment that terrorists are jealous of our open societies—our wealth, our freedom—and in fact count on that openness and our valuing of freedom to exploit us and damage us both economically and culturally. That may be true. But terrorists really count on cheap forms of communication. Mass media transforms a backwater movement into an international phenomenon. The twenty-four-hour news cycle turns a terrorist incident with a few deaths or injuries into a weeklong retrospective with a parade of pundits pontificating on every nuance until it feels as if there has been a weeklong string of terrorist attacks. The cascade of information (both real and "fake") overtakes our cognitive ability to process it, which likely intensifies our "threat" or "anxiety" response. Thus, on the one hand, we see ever intensifying hatred for all things Muslim, for example, and on the other we see documented cases of posttraumatic stress disorder (PTSD) resulting from terrorism news.[32] The ever-widening gap between the "threat" and the "anxiety" camps is leading to ever starker desired responses, such as Ted Cruz's famous "I don't know if sand can glow in the dark" comment[33] or then State Department spokesperson Marie Harf's comment "we just need to give terrorists jobs."[34]

## Communication, Recruiting, and the Weakness of the Terrorist Strategy

Terrorists are also becoming quite adept at using social media in conjunction with terrorist attacks to increase recruitment and fund-raising and as a form of communication with the broader world to influence our perception of risk.[35] Social media offer a cheap form of communication with wide global reach. For example, in 2011 approximately 17 million people in the Arab world were using Facebook in Arabic, and that number has almost certainly grown exponentially.[36] The breadth of access for terrorists is wide, allowing for remote recruiting and fund-raising far beyond that of earlier terrorist movements. And with active "Western foreign fighters" working for ISIS, the organization's reach has grown even more broadly throughout the Western world.[37]

By using images and videos to depict "warriors" in action and providing updates on the "war from the inside," terrorists attract attention to themselves and their cause and appeal to adventurers or sympathizers.[38] Slickly produced videos in English create an image of "wrongs" that must be "righted," which are used to recruit fighters from a much larger audience.[39] In several very important ways, social media provides the perfect vehicle for terrorists to communicate, coordinate, and recruit.[40]

First, the internet is widely available and becoming increasingly so. And it is becoming increasingly mobile, no longer tethered to land lines. The wide availability of access allows terrorists to transmit messages freely and quickly; they no longer have to recruit in a face-to-face fashion as in the past.[41] This new communication capability also facilitates more networked organization structures for terrorist organizations as discussed in Chapter 6.

Second, social media provide a platform for the transmission of information to rally support from the broader public. Most have seen the videos and photos posted from reported funerals of women and children who died at the hands of the imperialist invaders or due to the oppressive acts of an authoritarian regime. While videos and photos foster inductive leaps without context, images are powerful. And the broad access to these images and stories means that stories "go viral" quickly. The source of the information need not be well known or popular (consider the Russian government's recent attempts to interfere with the 2016 US election via Facebook and Twitter). Social media "democratizes" information sources, which means that almost anyone can participate.

Third, from an operational perspective, social media and mobile communications mean that almost anyone is a source of intelligence. In a scene in the movie *Black Hawk Down*, as the initial assault departs from base, a child herding sheep near the American base near Mogadishu, Somalia, uses a cell phone to alert the troops of warlord Mohamed Aidid to the incoming attack. The ease of access to and widespread adoption of mobile and internet technology around the world turn everyone into a potential intelligence agent (for good or bad).

Finally, terrorist organizations use social media to intimidate opponents and even brag about their exploits.[42] Al Shabab live-tweeted the killing of victims in Nairobi, Kenya, and Lashkar-e-Taiba used mobile technology and online applications such as Google Earth during its 2008 assault in Mumbai.[43] The use of social media has become so prolific that military leaders in the US Africa Command first learned of Ambassador John Christopher Stevens's death in the 9/11 anniversary attack on the US consulate in Benghazi, Libya, via a post on Twitter.[44] The role of social media and mobile technology has grown substantially, providing a platform for recruitment, a means to communicate with the broader public, a vehicle for intelligence gathering and coordination of activities, and a venue for intimidating opponents.

But information and communication can be a double-edged sword.[45] As sensationalized by the movie *Zero Dark Thirty*, communications can also be a weak link. Phone calls leave records, and websites and email leave digital footprints. Reliance on mobile technology makes terrorists both elusive and vulnerable at the same time. While electronic communication between key leaders of terrorist groups is minimized, there are other ways to track their movements and communications. And as the need for speed in communications increases, reliance on electronic methods to communicate will increase as well. As with the structural items discussed in Chapter 6, electronic communication is limited to that which is necessary only, representing a trade-off between speed of messaging and risk of detection.

## Concluding Remarks

The media remain an integral element of the fabric of Western society. That is both good and bad. Social/digital media have lowered communication costs, allowed media and news to reach a broader audience than ever before, and "democratized" information in a way previously unseen in the history of man. With a smart phone, we literally have the world's knowledge base at our fingertips. At the same time, though, we have also lowered the cost of communication for our enemies. Mobile access to the internet, twenty-four-hour news cycles with media conglomerates duking it out to scoop each other and fill their airtime with the day's most important news, and savvy, highly educated terrorists who can produce Hollywood-style propaganda have all conspired (directly or, most often, unknowingly) to inundate us with overwhelming volumes of images and news.

Governments engage in a delicate balancing act with terrorist use of media. On the one hand, terrorists reveal much intelligence about themselves and their tactics through their use of communications and media. On the other, allowing information to flow impacts consumers of information and generates (at least the terrorists hope) greater feelings of anxiety and elevated levels of risk aversion. How much is too much?

We also must be careful not to overlook the real power that government has when it manipulates information. Focusing our attention on "threats" associated with terrorism is powerfully tempting because, if successful, this allows governments to centralize and accumulate many resources that can be used for purposes not necessarily in the interests of citizens. Even if we assume that the government is acting in good faith, the natural accumulation of influence forms a tempting source of future power for people inclined to use it for less than honorable purposes.

Often overlooked in these discussions is the question of what role we as consumers of information play in this relationship. Do we bear some responsibility for how we consume and/or react to information? Of course we do. Although we are influenced by our natural responses to stimuli, as shown in Figure 7.1, how we ultimately react is still a choice. Seeking information outside our small circles of like-minded friends, for example, helps to temper our gut-level responses. But, ultimately, seeking more information is often costly (especially in terms of time), and so most people economize on that and fall into the habit of forming opinions based on very limited information, which is often skewed or biased.

So, then, how do we win the "information war" with terrorists? The overly simple answer is, with more information. Readers should understand something about themselves. How risk-averse are you? How do you react to perceived risks? With anxiety? With anger? Understanding that about ourselves helps us filter through information with a more skeptical, realistic view of how to interpret and react to it. Ample sources of data (many cited in this book) can be freely accessed if one wants to know more about terrorism. Engaging leaders armed with good information helps keep them honest (and less intellectually lazy) about the nature and risk of terrorism, but it also helps leaders understand the causes and levels of citizen concern.

From a broader view, information, media, and communications must become a central focus of counterterrorism operations. The recent controversy surrounding suspected Russian state interference in US elections (and elsewhere) highlights that more than small terrorist organizations are using media to their advantage. The risks exacerbated, if not introduced, by electronic media range from terrorist communications to state-level electronic warfare. Nevertheless, to win the information war we will likely have to think like our enemies and turn how they use media against them. We appear to be making strides in this domain but have a long way to go.

## Appendix to Chapter 7

Risk is a complex topic, in part because we base our decisions on interpretations of it. Risk aversion, however, focuses on how people view the benefits accruing from the outcome of risky events (or "gambles," in the wording of the literature). Here, we are interested in the marginal utility for a person of an additional dollar from a gamble. Let's focus on someone who is risk-averse.

In Figure 7.3, the *x*-axis represents the person's ending wealth after a gamble takes place, and the *y*-axis represents the "utility" of that wealth. The line in the figure is upward sloping, which means that this person gets more utility from more ending wealth. But notice that the line increases at a decreasing rate. This implies that each additional dollar increases the person's ending wealth, but its additional benefits decline. This is called the "decreasing marginal utility" of ending wealth. Not decreasing utility but decreasing marginal (change in) utility.

The straight line represents the potential outcomes of a gamble (in this case, let's think about the flip of a coin with two possible outcomes—heads or tails). If the coin is flipped and lands on heads, the person receives $W_1$ ending wealth. If the coin lands on tails, ending wealth is $W_2$. Before the coin is flipped, there is a 50/50 chance of either outcome, so the expected outcome, $E(W)$, is $E(W) = 0.5W_1 + 0.5W_2$. This is called the expected value. Moving horizontally from that point, we see that there is a utility of the expected wealth, or $U(E(W))$ in the figure.

**Figure 7.3    The Expected Utility and Certainty Equivalent
of a Gamble for a Risk-averse Person**

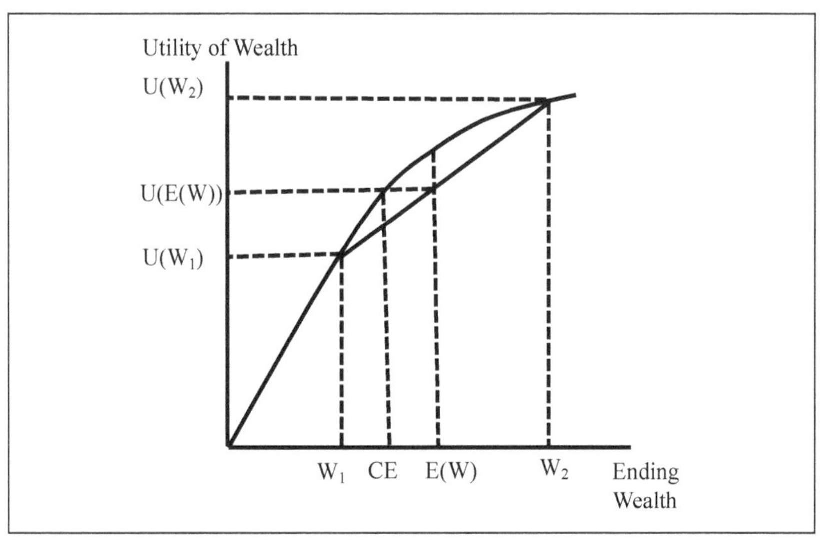


*Source*: Authors.

Where that horizontal line intersects the curved line creates another important point called the certainty equivalent (CE). The CE represents the ending wealth that this person would accept with certainty to avoid facing the gamble with the two outcomes ($W_1, W_2$). The difference between expected wealth $E(W)$ and the certainty equivalent (CE) is called the "risk premium." The is the amount of expected wealth that this person is willing to give up to get CE with certainty (not face the risk). This amount is, for example, an insurance premium. A person pays an insurance premium out of current income to guarantee receipt of at least CE no matter the outcome of the gamble. So you get your car replaced if you total it (CE). But if you do not have a wreck, you still have a valuable car and are only out the amount of the premium.

Of course, there is much more to the concept of risk aversion, but this simple explanation makes the critical point that as risk-averse individuals, we are likely to (rationally) give up some level of current benefits to protect ourselves against adverse outcomes. As the gamble becomes bigger (larger variability in outcomes) we will likely give up more current benefits. Understanding our risk aversion is critical to understanding how we are likely to respond to risky situations.

## Notes

1. Singman 2016.
2. Chapman University 2016.
3. Huddy et al. 2005.
4. Data from the Global Terrorism Database, University of Maryland.
5. Shaver 2015.
6. Viscusi 1990.
7. Johnson and Tversky 1983.
8. Yang, Coble, and Hudson 2009.
9. Some purists might argue that being consistently wrong is costly and that people will learn. That is likely true for frequent activities, such as food purchases. But for infrequent events such as terrorism, the lack of repetition makes learning much more difficult and costly.
10. Lahav 2004.
11. Cottman 1994.
12. McCann 1997.
13. This response, in part, may be because we (Americans and others) are generally more removed from the consequences of counterterrorism actions. Nevertheless, the anger-threat response is a motivating factor.
14. Herrmann, Tetlock, and Visser 1999.
15. Stewart, Ellingwood, and Mueller 2011.
16. Huddy, Khatib, and Capelos 2002.
17. Huddy et al. 2005.

18. Going back to the definition of terrorism as "political violence" in Chapter 2, appeasement is changing political outcomes to meet terrorist desires.

19. Weimann and Winn 1994.

20. Shane and Hubbard 2014.

21. Rohner and Frey 2007.

22. Kerry 2016.

23. Aldoory and Van Dyke 2006.

24. Brown 2003.

25. Gentzkow and Shapiro 2006.

26. Murray 2013; Haidt 2013.

27. Matusitz and Forrester 2013.

28. T. H. Post 2010.

29. Hudson and Lusk 2004.

30. Brummette, Zoch, and Miller 2013.

31. Vlahos, n.d.

32. Hamblen and Sloan 2016.

33. Glueck 2015.

34. *Fox News* 2015.

35. Shane and Hubbard 2014.

36. Ghannam 2011.

37. Klausen 2015.

38. Farwell 2014.

39. Mackey 2014.

40. R. Thompson 2011.

41. Watts 2008.

42. Greenwood 2013.

43. Beaumont 2008.

44. Klein 2014.

45. Farwell 2014.

8

# Four Critical Myths of Counterterrorism

Counterterrorism (CT) is perhaps as difficult to define as ter-
Counterterrorism (CT) is perhaps as difficult to define as terrorism itself. This is because it can use a multitude of modes—diplomacy, the military, law enforcement, and intelligence, for example—and can also follow many different strategies with many different short- and long-term goals. And, as with terrorism, the wide spectrum of possibilities often leads to many misconceptions and myths about what it is and how it works. This chapter focuses on four primary myths surrounding CT that are relevant to our understanding of how to combat terrorism, as well as potential implications of CT policies.

## Myth #1: A Coherent Counterterrorism Strategy Produces Predictable Responses

Popular television programming and the news (depending on the source) often give us the impression that there is an orchestrated response to terrorism across intelligence, military, and law enforcement organizations. We are told that the National Security Agency is listening to every conversation, giving us the sense that it can hear the plans and actions of future terrorists. The Central Intelligence Agency has embedded spies infiltrating terrorist networks around the world. The military is on guard, and clandestine Special Forces units are stalking terrorist leaders in the middle of the night. And all these diverse activities are being controlled tightly from a high-tech bunker in the Pentagon that can pinpoint terrorist targets with a GPS-guided Hellfire missile. The counterterrorism responses are often shown in isolated snippets, but pundits and spokespeople present the story of a well-oiled machine executing a solid, well-reasoned, and coherent terrorism strategy over time based on well-established models of behavior that precisely predict the outcome of any CT activity.

## Upon Further Review

While most people tend to associate the US "War on Terror" with the American response to the 9/11 attack, the United States has been engaged in an ongoing struggle with al-Qaeda and its associates since the mid-1990s, when the American intelligence community started to recognize that the leader of the organization, Osama bin Laden, was interested in expanding the jihadi struggle to Western targets, mainly the United States and Israel.[1] Interestingly, however, the American response to al-Qaeda's attacks prior to 9/11 was highly inconsistent. For example, following the 1998 car-bomb attacks against the American embassies in Dar es Salaam and Nairobi, which led to the complete destruction of the embassies and to more than two hundred fatalities, the United States responded by attacking al-Qaeda camps in Afghanistan and an al-Qaeda-associated factory in Sudan with Tomahawk cruise missiles.[2] Yet the United States decided not to respond at all following the attack against the USS *Cole* in 2000 in the port of Aden, when two al-Qaeda operatives crashed a boat loaded with explosive into the hull of the ship, causing the deaths of seventeen American sailors.[3] How can we explain this discrepancy? Is it just a matter of the differing number of casualties? Or the different types of target? Or, as some suggested, did the United States lack viable options for retaliation in 2000?

In fact, the same states and governments have exercised different responses to similar attacks in other instances. On June 25, 2006, Hamas attacked an Israeli military post near the Gaza Strip and kidnapped an Israeli soldier, Corporal Gilad Shalit. The Israeli government responded with a limited military operation in the southern part of the Gaza Strip as part of an attempted search and rescue operation that yielded no results. However, three weeks later, when Hezbollah ambushed an Israeli military patrol near the Israel-Lebanon border and kidnapped two Israeli soldiers, Israel responded with a massive military operation, initially using air power but later also ground forces in what became known as the Second Lebanon War.[4] Again, similar attacks led to the implementation of fundamentally different counterterrorism strategies, despite the operational similarities and the fact that in both cases the same government formulated the CT policies.

These examples reflect the nuanced and complicated nature of the policymaking process in the context of CT. Why, given very similar sets of operational circumstances, do similar events produce such disparate responses? Fundamentally, the idea that countries can execute some catch-all coherent CT strategy that is implemented consistently is more myth than reality. Of course, differences in domestic political situations, government preparation for differential responses, and the like, all play a role in response. But these facts further reinforce the idea that a coherent strategy is a unicorn in the mist. Another manifestation of this myth is the notion that we can predict with any degree of accuracy the response to any CT strategy.

The efforts to conceptualize and classify how countries respond to terrorism present multiple challenges for those seeking to understand CT. The high number of state institutions that take an active part in the shaping of the response to terrorism may confound those who hope to understand the decisionmaking process in this context—even if a coherent policy is in place in each state. In addition, the array of measures at states' disposal and the countless details of CT mechanisms that are not exposed to the public further undermine researchers' attempts to demarcate CT policies, strategies, and outcomes. These challenges have led CT scholars to adopt more basic frameworks, the most popular probably being the distinction between the war, legal, and reconciliatory models of counterterrorism.[5]

Table 8.1 presents the basic ingredients of counterterrorism models. The main criterion for distinguishing the different states' response is the identity of the main state agencies/proxies that execute the CT policies. The reconciliatory model defines terrorism as a political problem reflected in the inability of some political groups to access and operate within the political process. Therefore it includes measures exercised by politicians and diplomats and focuses on solving the terrorist threat by allowing these groups to gain more access to the political system or by directly engaging with their demands via negotiations and political reforms addressing the group's grievances.[6] Two other, more confrontational models focus on different aspects of violent CT policies. The war model defines terrorism as an act of war, suggesting the use of

**Table 8.1  Models of Counterterrorism**

| | War Model | Criminal Justice Model | Expanded Criminal Justice Model | Reconciliatory Model |
|---|---|---|---|---|
| The threat | Terrorism is an act of war | Terrorism is a crime | Terrorism is a "special" crime | Terrorism is a political problem |
| Aims and means | Elimination of terrorism | Arrest and penalization of terrorists while adhering to the "rule of law" | Use of special mechanisms for penalization and preventing terrorism that generally stretch democratic acceptability | Addressing the root causes of terrorism |
| Constitutional and legal aspects | Laws of war dictate counterterrorism measures; consequently any constitutional or legal consideration is secondary | The state responds to terrorist incidents in compliance with state criminal law and is subject to constant judiciary regulation | Special legislation grants more powers to authorities and limits the legal rights of those accused of terrorism | Corresponds with the law such that no real new legislation is needed and only current laws are applied to new situations |
| Agents | Intelligence and military units | Police and the criminal justice system | Police, police special forces, and the criminal justice system | Policymakers, brokers, and diplomats |

operational and legal military mechanisms, while the criminal justice model perceives terrorism as a criminal act and endorses a response via the traditional law enforcement system, including using the judicial and justice systems, state advocacy, and conventional policing operations.[7]

The use of these models as an analytical tool has declined since the 2000s for several conceptual and operational reasons. First, scholars frequently acknowledge that focusing on operative aspects of the CT response leads to neglect of other factors involved in the fight against terrorism, particularly issues related to the political and legal systems in which these policies are created.[8] For example, in many cases a variety of legislative initiatives intended to provide a more convenient operational environment for military forces can accompany a war model. The adaptations of the British antiterrorism acts during the struggles against the Irish Republican Army (IRA) in the 1970s and 1980s are a case in point.[9] The continuous evolution of strategies reflects the reality that the models suffer from limited resolution, which makes attribution of some types of CT policies to a specific model challenging. Researchers tried to partially resolve this predicament by developing a tertiary model posited between the military and criminal justice models, that is, the expanded criminal justice model, which includes measures such as the use of semimilitary police forces, administrative detentions, and legal prescription of political movements.[10]

Probably the main reason for the declining utility of the models relates to the fact that contemporary CT policies are almost always multifaceted and include the simultaneous use of elements from multiple models. To illustrate, during the second Palestinian uprising, Israeli authorities implemented military measures while also maintaining an open channel of communication with the Palestinian National Authority and negotiating steps to reduce the violence.[11] In response to the 9/11 attacks, the United States initiated comprehensive military operations in Afghanistan while at the same time recalibrating domestic CT efforts with the introduction of various measures that corresponded with the "expanded criminal justice model" and enhanced law enforcement capabilities. These included, for example, increased limits on terrorism suspects' rights and the use of more intrusive surveillance mechanisms.[12]

Importantly, the growing multi- and bilateral cooperation in CT operations also limits the utility of the traditional models. The increasing tendency of some contemporary terrorist groups, such as ISIS and al-Qaeda, to operate globally using a cellular network structure has forced the responding countries to develop complex mechanisms of cooperation and coordination. A recent study, for example, identified more than 170 cases of bilateral cooperation in the area of CT, both kinetic and nonkinetic.[13] Thus, any discussion of CT strategies in the modern era must include these cooperative models of government response.

## Myth #2: Military Force Is Ineffective in Counterterrorism

*In a narrow sense, Jeremy Corbyn's assertion that Britain's recent military interventions have increased the risk of terror attacks in the UK is widely accepted. Many would say it's a statement of the blindingly obvious.*

—James Robbins[14]

Based on casual observation, any reasonable person would conclude that despite military interventions in the "War on Terror," terrorism has actually increased. This seems so widely accepted that one wonders why we would question it.[15] Indeed, the literature on CT is somewhat skeptical about the utility of military measures in the fight against terrorism. The perception that CT is also a war of ideas has engendered a school of thought holding that in fighting ideological groups, we cannot rely just on brute force but must also counter their ideological dispersion.[16] Hence, by discrediting their political agenda via strategic communication efforts, as well as countering their ability to disseminate their ideology and recruit effectively, we can deprive terrorist organizations in the long term of crucial resources such as new members and societal support. An additional popular argument against the use of military measures focuses on the perception that the use of military forces against organizations operating in urban areas, whose operatives are in many cases indistinguishable from the civilian population, is likely to produce collateral damage, which in turn discredits the CT efforts and helps terrorist groups mobilize additional domestic and international support.[17]

To support the assertion that military operations may deal with the symptoms of terrorism but not with its root causes and are thus ineffective in the long term, policymakers and scholars point to a long list of military efforts that failed to eliminate terrorist campaigns. Some prominent case studies analyzed to illustrate the limitations of military force in CT were the French failure to defeat the National Liberation Front in Algeria,[18] which led to the withdrawal of all French military forces from the colony in 1964; the failure of Israel to eliminate Palestinian militant organizations, despite its massive investment in maintaining its military control in the West Bank;[19] and the ongoing failure of Western coalitions in Afghanistan and Iraq to terminate campaigns by groups affiliated with the global jihadi movement and the Taliban.[20]

## Upon Further Review

A reexamination of the literature and case studies of military operations in the context of CT can lead to more nuanced conclusions. Actually, in some cases, military measures not only reduced terrorism to sustainable levels but eliminated armed resistance completely. In Sri Lanka in 2007, the Liberation Tigers of Tamil Eelam (LTTE), traditionally considered one of the most capable and effective terrorist organizations on the planet, still controlled large swaths of territory in the northern and eastern parts of the island. This organization promoting the political liberation of the Tamil population managed to create a state-like entity in these areas and provide various services to the local Tamil population (note the similarity to other long-standing groups, such as Hamas, in this respect). Despite a formal cease-fire agreement between the LTTE and the Sinhalese government, the latter started to intensify its military pressure on the organization in the fall of 2007. Gradually, the LTTE's lines of defense collapsed, and the territory under its control shrank. On May 17, 2009, the last LTTE stronghold surrendered, and the Sinhalese government announced a military victory.[21]

Similar dynamics characterized the defeat by Russian military forces in the late 1990s of separatists aspiring to establish an independent Islamic state in Chechnya and Dagestan. In the summer and fall of 1999, Chechen militias led by Shamil Basayev and Saudi-born cleric Ibn al-Khattab invaded Dagestan and captured several villages. This reflected jihadi Chechens' desire to unite the Muslim population in the Caucasus under one Islamic polity. The Russian Federation's forces pushed the militias back to Chechnya in the early fall, just to witness the Chechens retaliating with a series of terrorist attacks against civilian targets in Dagestan. In response, the new Russian prime minister, Vladimir Putin, ordered a military campaign to reclaim full control of Chechnya, which was achieved in May 2000. In early 2002, Russia formally ended the military phase of the operation, having reached a sustainable security situation.[22] And while some separatist groups remained active until the end of the decade, very few will deny the operational effectiveness of the Russian offensive, which broke the backbone of the Chechen separatist Islamic movement.

Lastly, when in 2002 Hamas intensified its suicide attack campaign against Israeli civilian and military targets, the Israeli government responded by redeploying military forces in main Palestinian urban areas in the West Bank, as well as by initiating a massive campaign of targeted killings of major Palestinian military operatives. Indeed, by 2005 the infrastructure of Hamas in the West Bank had been reduced mainly to its political association, and it was not able to continue the violent struggle; thus the organization shifted the center of its operations to the Gaza Strip.[23]

These case studies suggest that several conditions might facilitate the effectiveness of a military response as the main driving force of CT policy. The most obvious is the existence of "on-the-ground" military infrastructure, which provides clear and obvious goals for a military campaign. In other words, a significant portion of the operational assets of the terrorist organization is vulnerable to direct military attacks. The eventual collapse of ISIS in Iraq and the elimination of most of the Shining Path's infrastructure in Peru are further examples of this dynamic.[24]

Additionally, organizations concentrated in a specific territory that adopt a paramilitary hierarchical structure seem more vulnerable to military-based CT efforts for several reasons. First, the concentration of most members of the organization in specific regions allows the state to minimize collateral damage and isolates the negative impact of a military response to specific segments of the population. For example, when the Canadian government initiated martial law in Quebec in October 1970 in order to end the terrorist campaign of the Front for the Liberation of Quebec, the government avoided substantial public backlash because other parts of Canada were isolated from the harsh measures implemented in the French-speaking territory of the country.[25] Second, by developing a paramilitaristic organizational structure and culture, the terrorist organization gives up some of the basic advantages of engaging in asymmetric conflict, especially terrorism, including the ability to adapt quickly to changes in the security environment and to effectively blend into the civilian population. Lastly, military campaigns, especially in democracies, seem mainly feasible against terrorist organizations that represent minority groups (Palestinians, Tamils, Kurds, Francophones, etc.). The fact that the impacted population is a minority, representing a distinct culture and/or ethnicity, helps the government to portray the conflict as partially against foreign elements that threaten national solidarity and the territorial integrity of the state and to legitimize means usually deemed unacceptable in democratic political frameworks.

The discussion above illustrates the need for a more accurate and rigorous analysis of CT campaigns. We do not argue that a military response is preferable to or more advantageous than other CT measures or that it is unequivocally suitable against specific types of groups in all situations. Moreover, the use of military forces in CT campaigns raises significant ethical and moral issues. But under specific conditions it can be uniquely attractive to policymakers, as well as fairly effective, and should not be dismissed out of hand as either leading to more terrorism or ineffective as a CT strategy.

## Myth #3: Democracies Need Not Give Up Liberty to Protect Themselves Against Terrorism

*Those who would give up essential liberty to purchase a little temporary safety, deserve neither liberty nor safety.*
—Benjamin Franklin

Citizens of the United States and other Western democracies fancy themselves exceptional based on their inclusive governments and codified limitations on the power of government in individuals' lives (especially in the United States and other nations with written constitutions). With some justification, they believe that they have created systems of government that protect individual liberties and allow self-determination. The literature and the policy discussion regarding CT tend to devote significant effort to understanding and exploring the ethical and normative challenges that democracies face when developing CT policies. Simply put, because the struggle against terrorism in many cases involves engagement with civilian populations, democracies need to balance their desire to increase their control and monitoring of the population (to identify and prevent potential terrorist attacks) with their commitment to maintaining fundamental liberal and democratic norms such as the right to privacy and free expression.[26] The belief that the response to terrorism should not change "who we are" is common in Western countries. But is that even possible?

### Upon Further Review

Scholars tend to point out several specific risks associated with the expansion of state powers to fight terrorism, including the risk of creating a legal and operational slippery slope, of a potential increase in mistrust of government authorities and agencies, especially when the

CT policies target specific minority groups within society, and of spillover effects into other domains of the criminal justice system.[27] One should keep in mind a couple of important dynamics that have solidified in the last couple decades. First, while this freedom/security debate is important and should inform ongoing governments' formulation of CT policies, it seems empirically less and less relevant in the current security landscape. Second, many participants in this debate seem to ignore the mass integration of new technologies into law enforcement work, which inherently impacts the way governments monitor the civilian population even without the presence of terrorism or CT policies.

As for the first point, it is almost impossible to currently identify a Western democracy that has not abandoned the pure criminal justice model within given civil liberty constraints and shifted toward more effective security at the expense of democratic civil liberties in the last couple decades. For example, in many Western democracies CT legislation allows the use of special courts with some limitations on due process and expands the conditions under which government agencies can conduct searches and surveillances of people and their personal records. Moreover, in most Western democracies, limitations on the freedoms of organizations and of movement are now part of the CT legislation, especially with regard to associations that promote militant and nonmainstream political and social views.

To explore this trend more effectively, it seems useful to use a two-dimensional space to identify the types of policies implemented by states to counter terrorism. This "space of response" utilizes two vectors:[28] legal measures and kinetic/operational measures (Figure 8.1).

The right upper square (A) of the "space of response" includes situations that give prominence to a hard-line struggle both in the legal and the operative arenas. The lower right quadrant (B) represents situations that include a hard-line response in the operative dimension along with a lower-key response on the legal level. The upper left quadrant (C) represents the inverse situation, in which there is broad legal authorization to take actions against terrorism; yet the forces deployed are standard law enforcement agencies. Finally, the lower left quadrant (D) indicates situations that typically feature in states that endure infrequent or limited terrorism. In these situations, standard law enforcement forces usually carry out countermeasures, and antiterrorism legislation is limited.

The data suggest that out of eighty-three democracies, just 22 percent never enacted legislation enhancing the CT powers of law enforcement in a way that undermines some democratic practices (quadrant D). These are mostly countries that do not suffer from a significant threat

## Figure 8.1   The "Space of Response" to Terrorism

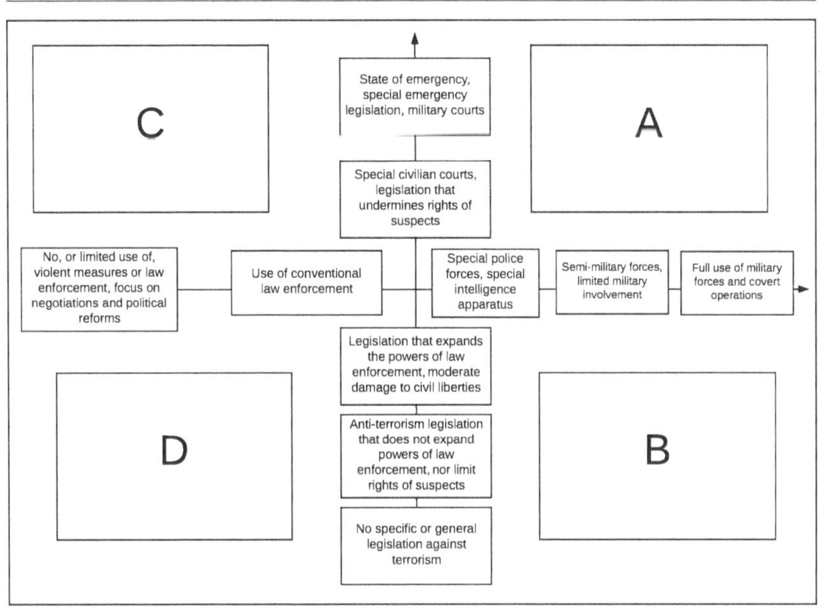


*Source:* Perliger 2012b.

of terrorism, such as Switzerland or Norway. In contrast, 24 percent of democracies utilized both harsh legal and kinetic measures (quadrant A). Additionally, 46 percent exercised just severe legal measures (quadrant B), and 7.2 percent just severe kinetic measures (quadrant C). The latter two groups reflect the tendency of democracies to first put in place a legal framework that allows them to eventually enhance the power of state agencies.

These findings confirm that virtually all democracies facing terrorism-related threats utilized various measures to enhance their CT capabilities, mainly by providing additional legal tools to their law enforcement and limiting the rights of terrorism suspects (think PATRIOT Act here); in rarer cases they also preferred to use military measures. Considering this tendency, it seems important to advance the discourse beyond examination of the ethical aspects of the expansion of the criminal justice model and also to attempt to identify why we see such broad similarities in the way democracies respond to the terrorist threat and the implications of this trend in terms of the ability of democracies to maintain their normative and ethical core values.

A second important development relates to the role of technology and data in the implementation of CT policies. With the growing use of various technological platforms for recruitment, communication, and dissemination of operational knowledge, terrorist organizations are able today to expand their geographical reach, coordinate their efforts, and more effectively mobilize support (recall Chapter 7). However, at the same time, the use of technological platforms also potentially renders them more visible and exposed, especially as law enforcement enhances its ability to exploit online platforms for intelligence gathering and monitoring of suspects. At the same time, the use of technology also raises a plethora of new ethical dilemmas regarding the balance between civil liberties and security, which will require ongoing analysis and political debate.

## Myth #4: We Don't and Shouldn't Negotiate with Terrorists

As terrorism increasingly became a staple of international and domestic politics, two major schools of thoughts evolved with regard to conciliatory policies. The first can be summarized by a phrase used by many policymakers in the last seventy years: "we do not negotiate with terrorists." President George W. Bush, for example, refused to engage in any negotiations with al-Qaeda and the Taliban following the invasion to Afghanistan, even though some from within the latter were willing to cooperate in the establishment of a new democratic system in the country.[29] Bush famously declared, "The only way to deal with these people is to bring them to justice. You can't talk to them. You can't negotiate with them."[30] Similarly, when asked in 1985 about potential negotiations with the Palestinian Liberation Organization (PLO), Israeli defense minister Yitzhak Rabin replied, "The PLO is a terrorist organization with whom there is no point in even deluding ourselves into thinking we can negotiate."[31] The major argument justifying such an approach is usually that negotiations legitimize the use of violence to advance political goals and thus may encourage other political groups to resort to the tactic. Additionally, many have pointed out, a conciliation process in many cases allows the terrorist organization to regroup and eventually renew its attacks from a better position.[32] Lastly, negotiations can be effective only when terrorists are willing to moderate and negotiate; thus, such a policy approach is almost impossible to implement with revolutionary groups attempting to entirely delegitimize the existing political system.

The second school of thought advocates conciliation, usually as an effective tool for dealing with the root causes of the threat rather than just the symptoms (as is the case with the more violent models of CT). In addition, supporters of conciliation note that it can encourage other groups to negotiate and that members of groups involved in negotiations usually moderate. The main assumption is that during its nonviolent phase the group will undergo structural changes that will make returning to a violent path difficult. Lastly, conciliation limits harm to civil liberties and collateral damage, as well as provides further legitimacy to violent response if that is eventually necessary.[33] Most enduring conflicts between terrorist groups and state actors usually include phases of direct or mediated negotiations between the adversaries. In contrast to other models of CT, conciliation includes several unique features. It is usually led by politicians and diplomats, and they, not the operational agents of the state, interact with the terrorists (which is not the case in other models of response). Moreover, the conciliatory approach assumes that terrorism reflects the inability of specific constituencies to gain access to the political process and thus aims to allow the groups to express their grievances and to negotiate a mechanism that will allow them to play an active role in the political system. In this sense, the conciliatory approach treats terrorism as a political problem to be addressed with political tools.

## Upon Further Review

Do these two options really pose a dilemma? We argue that empirical examination of most enduring conflicts reflects several major trends. First, almost always the immediate response to a terrorist campaign includes some implementation of military or criminal justice tools. Policymakers have limited incentive to concede to the terrorists' demands or to negotiate in the early stages of the conflict when there are no indications that the terrorists can maintain an enduring campaign and increase the costs for the state. Second, escalation in the state response will occur when there is a rise in the symbolic or psychological impact of the attacks.[34] Such an increase is usually associated with attacks against highly symbolic targets (such as against political leaders or institutions), high-casualty attacks, or the use of force multipliers such as suicide bombers. In these instances, political leaders may experience growing concern about their ability to maintain political stability or the legitimacy of their rule, as well as anxiety that the organization's attacks will demonstrate its resilience and commitment. Finally, if the escalation does not lead to satisfactory results, we may see a willingness on the part of the government to negotiate with the group or independently implement political reforms to reduce the terrorists' motivation to continue their violent struggle.

The processes described above imply that only enduring conflicts lead to negotiations and that escalation will almost always precede them. Indeed, twenty years of struggle with Palestinian terrorism and a dramatic rise in Palestinian violence in the West Bank (also known as the "First Intifada") in the late 1980s and early 1990s led both Israel and the PLO to agree in 1993 to initiate a conciliation process that included direct negotiations.[35] Similarly, escalation in the violence in Northern Ireland in the early 1990s, especially in the area of South Armagh, where IRA snipers inflicted casualties on British forces, as well as the new ability of the IRA to shoot down helicopters, led to initial negotiations that resulted in two cease-fire agreements and eventually to the 1998 Good Friday Agreement.[36] Interestingly, despite Sinn Féin members' willingness to negotiate in the mid-1980s, Jerry Adams, leader of the party, believed that just another decade of violence would ultimately convince the British to begin negotiations.

Similar dynamics characterize even cases in which negotiations are unsuccessful. In early 2000 the LTTE increased its offensive against the Sinhalese government in Sri Lanka. LTTE not only expanded the areas under its control in northern Sri Lanka but also produced a series of successful suicide attacks, including one at the Bandaranaike International Airport, which destroyed eight military aircraft. The situation was so severe that tourism plummeted, and as a result the economy suffered negative growth for the first time since Sri Lanka gained its independence. A counterresponse by special forces of the Sri Lankan military, which included the assassination of several top LTTE commanders, eventually led to mutual exhaustion and a memorandum of agreement and cease-fire in February 2002. The cease-fire eventually collapsed and led to a military campaign that resulted in the collapse of the LTTE in May 2009.[37]

Several parameters, however, can prevent negotiations despite willingness from one side. Enduring conflicts will not include strategic negotiations (in contrast to tactical ones, for example, with regard to hostage exchanges) when the ideological discrepancy does not allow meaningful concessions. Thus, jihadi groups, who see any cooperation with infidels as a direct violation of their rigid ideological framework, are not potential partners in a conciliation process, despite the fact that the jihadi "global struggle" is entering its fourth decade. Similarly, Communist groups in western Europe were never candidates for negotiation as a result of the revolutionary absolutism of their ideological agenda. Moreover, when the terrorism is not grounded in a domestic dispute and the group lacks a cohesive constituency, policymakers have limited incentives to engage in a conciliation process because the violence usually lacks the potential to impact on the legitimacy of the ruling elites/parties. Thus negotiations are rare between nation-states and actors without a specific local (geographic) base, such as al-Qaeda or global environmental groups.

We can conclude that rather than resulting from a holistic decision-making process, conciliation in the context of CT is usually a product of long-term attrition combined with additional specific conditions that provide incentives for decisionmakers to adopt a conciliatory approach. Conciliation with terrorists, while still fairly unpopular among the general publics of most democracies, seems almost inherent to most enduring conflicts that involve state and substate actors and thus must remain an arrow in the quiver of CT policy.

## A Defensive Approach

One may have noticed that, so far, most CT measures that we have discussed, except perhaps the conciliation model, have been offensive in nature, meaning that they were based on violent and direct interactions between state agencies and terrorists. Indeed, most of the academic and policy literature focuses primarily on kinetic operations aiming to eliminate or undermine terrorists' operational capabilities, whether via direct attacks against them and their infrastructure or by enhancing the powers of law enforcement and intelligence agencies (increasing the "costs of production" of terrorism discussed in Chapters 2 and 7). Nonetheless, a less noticeable stream of studies has also examined the utility of defensive approaches for CT.

Some studies, for example, have identified the advantages of physical barriers as a quick solution to specific types of terrorism. To illustrate, when during 2002 militant Palestinian organizations produced multiple high-casualty suicide attacks every month in Israel's urban centers, the Israeli government approved the erection of a barrier between the West Bank and Israel. By early 2004, large parts of the barrier (or the "Separation Fence," as Israeli authorities termed it, despite many of its sections being concrete wall) were completed. The impact was noticeable. In 2004 and 2005 the number of suicide attacks declined dramatically, and while not solely responsible for this, the barrier significantly elevated the difficulties and costs involved in producing suicide attacks inside Israeli population centers.[38] Similarly, as the use of vehicle-driven IEDs (i.e., car bombs) became more popular in places such as Afghanistan and Iraq in the mid-2000s, the coalition forces in these countries realized the importance of creating physical barriers, which facilitated the formation of safe zones. Physical barriers are not long-term solutions, are costly, and definitely present a set of normative/moral and operational challenges. Nonetheless, they can provide a short-term defensive solution.

Another stream of studies focused on the management and prevention of attacks, particularly in urban settings. If the effectiveness of terrorism depends on its ability to generate substantial psychological impact, preventive measures and effective management of the site of an attack can undermine the overall direct and psychological consequences of terrorist attacks. Probably the most obvious example of the potential of such an approach is the disappearance of aviation terrorism. If in the 1960s and the 1970s the hijacking of civilian aircrafts was one of the more popular and effective methods used by terrorist groups, the introduction of preventive measures in international flights pushed the terrorists to look for different targets. Following the exercise of such measures also in domestic flights in the United States after 9/11, aviation terrorism has practically become an artifact of the history of terrorism rather than a prominent contemporary terrorist tactic. Similarly, the decision of some countries to introduce preventive safety measures in indoor public facilities also proved effective. The Israeli government decided in 2002 that every public facility in the entertainment and food industries must ensure the presence of guards as well as searches of patrons' belongings, leading to a substantial decline in attacks against targets such as shopping malls and restaurants.[39]

Sometimes, however, terrorist attacks cannot be prevented, so effective response and coordination between all first and secondary responders becomes crucial to limit the overall direct and psychological impact of the attack. A growing number of studies have identified how synchronization, coordination, and effective communication among all responders at attack sites can directly impact the ultimate number of casualties, as well as the time required to return activities to normal.[40]

To summarize, the discussion so far reflects several important distinctions between offensive and defensive CT. First, national/federal authorities execute offensive responses almost exclusively, while state, regional, and local agencies also carry out defensive CT operations. Therefore, coordination and collaboration in defensive operations can be more challenging and complicated. Second, while offensive CT strives to eliminate the infrastructure of terrorist organizations, defensive measures, aside from attempting to limit the efficacy of terrorist attacks, focus on limiting the indirect effects (i.e., psychological, social, and political) of terrorism on the population and policymakers. Lastly and importantly, while offensive measures focus on striking at terrorists and limiting their operational capabilities, defensive measures concentrate on protecting the civilian population. Therefore, successful implementation of defensive measures demands sensitivity to and understanding of the needs and vulnerabilities of the civilian population.

## Concluding Remarks

As in the realm of terrorism, a good many myths swirl around in the realm of counterterrorism and likely prevent clearheaded analysis of CT alternatives and effectiveness among the public and policymakers. Unfortunately, to expect that CT activities will always produce predictable and controllable responses is simply unrealistic. There are simply too many variables out of the control of experts. But it is reasonable to expect our policymakers to develop and work toward a CT strategy that is flexible and responsive to changes in the operational environment and also consistent with our values and longer-term objectives. To accomplish this, however, we must recognize that added security comes at a price. We must also recognize that removing options from the arsenal of weapons (e.g., negotiations or military force) will not make the job any easier.

## Notes

1. Coll 2004; Wright 2006.
2. P. Thompson 2004.
3. Burnett 2003.
4. Perliger 2012b.
5. Pedahzur and Ranstorp 2001; Sederberg 1995; Crelinsten and Schmid 1992.
6. Sederberg 1995; Schmid 1988.
7. Crelinsten 1998; Bremer 1992; Pedahzur and Ranstorp 2001.
8. Perliger 2012b.
9. Bonner 2000.
10. Pedahzur and Ranstorp 2001.

11. Schulze 2001.

12. Howell 2003.

13. Kinetic refers to active engagement with a terrorist target, whereas nonkinetic relates to information sharing, joint training, and joint intelligence operations. Perliger and Milton 2018.

14. Robbins 2017.

15. Greenslade 2015.

16. Cohen 2003; Freeman 2004.

17. Blankenship 2018; Crenshaw 1981.

18. Towers 2002.

19. Pedahzur and Perliger 2010.

20. Thrall and Groepner 2017; Chesney 2005.

21. Battle 2010; de Silva 2012.

22. Kramer 2005; Lapidus 2002.

23. Esposito 2005; Robinson 2010.

24. In the case of the Shining Path, locally organized peasant organizations largely shouldered the military operations in cooperation with and backed militarily by the government of Peru.

25. Perliger 2012b.

26. Schmid 1992; Wilkinson 1977.

27. Crelinsten and Schmid 1992; Perliger, Hasisi, and Pedahzur 2009; Wheeler 2017.

28. Perliger 2012b.

29. Coll 2018.

30. Toros 2008.

31. Browne and Dickson 2010.

32. Wilkinson 1977.

33. Sederberg 1995; Neumann 2007; Clutterbuck 1992.

34. Perliger 2012b.

35. Bishara 1998; Pearlman 2011.

36. Hayes and McAllister 1999; Bew 2007.

37. de Silva 2012.

38. Pedahzur and Perliger 2010.

39. Pahran, Pedahzur, and Perliger 2005.

40. Perliger, Pedahzur, and Zalmanovitch 2005; Hills 2002; Perry 2003.

# 9

# Putting It All in Perspective

ney through the field of terrorism studies. Along the way, we've tried to debunk common myths about terrorism such as that we can attribute terrorists' behavior to religious fundamentalism, mental illness, ignorance, or extreme poverty. We also addressed common misperceptions about terrorist organizations, demonstrating that their organizational designs and use of media are intentional. The previous chapter unearthed some myths about counterterrorism (CT), demonstrating both the complexity of CT strategy and the areas in which existing strategies have succeeded or come up short. Our purpose has not been, in most cases, to plow new academic ground; however, at times, we have synthesized scientific literature in new ways to help illuminate ideas and stimulate thinking about how terrorism interfaces with aspects of social and economic processes as well as your everyday life.

After such a journey, it is usually helpful to step back and take a look at the forest and not just the trees. What conclusions can we draw? How does this information help us make sense of our complex world? Of course, we have not answered all the questions. And, quite frankly, we never could. In fact, in many places, we have only scratched the surface of complex problems, but we have offered a very thorough set of academic references so that interested readers can delve into the scientific literature if they so desire.

We can draw a couple of very broad lessons from the literature and logic surrounding terrorism. These are associated with several key factors: the supply and demand for terrorism; the "optimal" amount of terrorism; the complexity of the human brain and behavior and their role in terrorism; the role of technology in terrorism; and the need to think innovatively about CT.

## The Supply and Demand for Terrorism

Terrorist organizations produce political violence. From an economic perspective, nothing special differentiates terrorism per se from other products, such as corn or computers. There are producers of terrorism, and these producers have a cost of production (a supply curve). And there are demanders of terrorism, and these demanders receive some sort of benefit (a demand curve). These costs and benefits need not be measured in terms of money, although money is often involved. CT has long focused on the supply side of terrorism. That is, we wish to increase the "cost of production" of terrorism such that, given a level demand, the "price" rises and reduces the quantity of terrorism produced.

Contrary to some commonly held beliefs, we have been relatively successful in this activity. This is not to say that terrorists have not shifted production technologies (IEDs, for example, became a popular tactic in Afghanistan and then were adopted in Iraq) to lower the costs again. That is the nature of CT: we raise costs; they find new ways to lower costs. But, overall, terrorism has become costlier to execute.

We have been much less successful (and, dare we say, inattentive) in dealing with the demand for terrorism. What causes people to want to perpetrate or orchestrate terrorist activities? A good portion of this book points out that what people think drives demand (or participation) in terrorism is generally wrong. Terrorists are not crazy, poor, or particularly ideological; nor are financiers of terrorism. At least the evidence we have to date says these notions are generally myths.

In many cases, the seeming causes of terrorism are really just symptoms of a more pervasive disease: weak institutions. The case of poverty and terrorism is maybe the clearest example in which the same corrupt, unequal institutions that destroy economies and disincentivize investment in education also create an environment in which political violence, even terrorism, is one of the few reliable mechanisms of change. Similarly, when societal institutions break down, the uncertainty created through unemployment, nonexistent health-care systems, and government turmoil drives individuals to seek out groups that offer a sense of stability. For some, family is the answer; for others, religious groups; for others, politically active terrorist groups. The more severe the breakdown of institutions, the more appealing these groups become.

Of course, an astute reader may say that strong institutions do not matter where caliphates and sharia law reign. These are also institutions, after all, and are wholly inconsistent with Western ideals of freedoms of the press and religion and separation of church and state. True, but we are arguing that nominally secular states (or "moderate Muslim" states) with weak social and economic institutions are a ripe environment for terrorists wishing to establish those caliphates. When a state, for example, does not or cannot aggressively protect freedom of religion, this opens the door for the dominance of violent religious groups. Afghanistan prior to the Taliban was a very different place than it was after the Taliban.

In reality, then, neither creating more jobs nor teaching religious tolerance will reduce terrorism significantly as poverty and religious fundamentalism are not primary drivers. But weak institutions open the door for those factors to then influence the development of political/ social movements that may become violent. That does not mean, however, that no other paths will benefit local populations and reduce the demand for terrorism. Promoting economic liberalization and increasing government legitimacy through participatory processes have both been shown to increase economic well-being and therefore reduce at least one component of grievance that may give rise to support for terrorism (either through tacit collusion or outright participation). So, it is not the poverty per se that causes terrorism but the weak institutions that lead to increased grievances and people seeking ways to redress them. And when governments are weak and nonparticipatory, actors may choose more violent means to seek political change.

These issues are too complex for further in-depth discussion here. We hope that readers will appreciate the importance of understanding why people might demand terrorism. A better understanding of the why will more likely lead to rational CT policies that serve to reduce both the demand for and the supply of terrorism in the long run.

## The Optimal Amount of Terrorism

The discussion above leads to a natural question: Is the optimal amount of terrorism zero? Before we get to an answer, it might be worth considering another "bad" in society: pollution. Everyone agrees pollution is undesirable, and as a whole we are willing to make sacrifices to reduce it, such as paying a little more for clean energy or mass transit systems. But we all have our limits in this regard. We are likely unwilling to forgo all electricity to eliminate all pollution related to producing that electricity, and we likely would rather not give up our cell phones to prevent the pollution created during the mining of nickel or lithium for their batteries.

What does that have to do with terrorism? Plenty. While the emotional answer to the "how much terrorism is optimal" question is typically "none," the best answer is almost certainly "a little." Figure 9.1 illustrates.

The marginal benefit (think demand) for the abatement (think CT) of terrorism is downward sloping. That is, at very high "prices" for abatement, we do not expect much demand. However, as the price decreases, more abatement is demanded. Conversely, the marginal cost (supply) of abatement is upward sloping. In fact, as the quantity of abatement rises, the costs often rise exponentially. This is because getting that next terrorist just becomes harder and harder. The willingness to pay for abatement is not infinite, and so as we decide how to allocate scarce resources, we must decide how much cost we are willing to shoulder. This will almost never equate to total abatement (zero terrorism). Therefore, we have an "acceptable" or "optimal" level of terrorism, which

## Figure 9.1   The Costs and Benefits of Terrorism Abatement

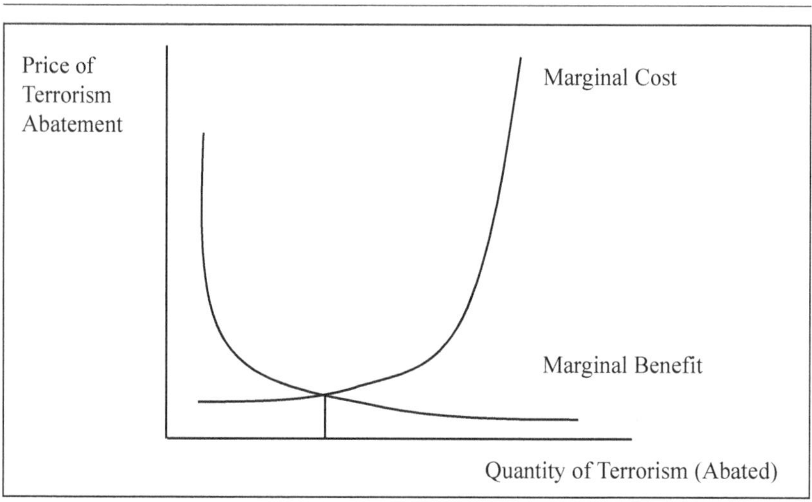


*Source:* Authors.

sounds a bit morbid, perhaps, but economically rational. So the high-sounding rhetoric of "paying any price" to end terrorism should remain just that: rhetoric. In reality ending terrorism is neither economically desirable nor feasible. But we can influence the shape of those curves (think back to Chapter 7 and our willingness to pay under risk) and therefore increase or decrease the level of terrorism.

## Human Complexity and Terrorism

We have difficulty understanding the "demand" for terrorism or the willingness to support and fund CT efforts in part because doing so relies on our understanding of people, and, well, people are compli-cated. As we saw in Chapter 5, terrorists are not crazy in any reliably definable way. This conclusion is disconcerting. Ascribing such heinous acts to mental instability is much more comfortable than explaining them with rational logic.

The literature has shown us that stress and hunger alter our responses to stimuli.[1] Biochemical responses to these environmental factors change our brain functions and generate different decisions. This is also disconcerting as it means we have less ability to explain decisions based on "rationality" because different environmental factors can lead to different "rational" choices.

Further complicating things is our woeful lack of understanding of other factors at play. For example, early research shows that factors such as prenatal stress in a mother impacts the hormonal development of a fetus, and hormonal differences carry forward and impact the responses of the eventual adults. Could a famine result in a spike in conflict and terrorism twenty years later? This is plausible, but the research is far too nascent to yield a definitive answer. Nevertheless, human complexity clearly makes our understanding of the motivations for terrorism and CT demand less certain or precise.

## The Changing Role of Technology in Terrorism and CT

This conclusion seems so obvious as to be almost cliché. However, the general public has less awareness about this issue than one would think. The recent potential impact of "bots" and "paid trolls" on US elections is a good example. People were likely at least partially manipulated without their awareness and, judging by polling on the matter, without their belief even afterward.

Chapter 7 tries to show how information (false or otherwise) can cascade through a social network and how that affects our thinking about topics. In particular, with terrorism, our risk aversion coupled with this information can substantially impact our thinking, and both terrorists and governments know it. Clearly, social media technology accelerates and broadens information diffusion. But should rational actors not be able to filter the wheat from the chaff? That is, will we not figure out what information is correct and how to act on it? Perhaps over time, but only if bad information results in bad decisions that are observable after the fact—that is, you can see and learn from your mistake. That is a heroic assumption in a digital age when we pass along information via social media with little personal consequence, even though the consequences for the group may be dire.

As we also saw in Chapter 7, if you live by Facebook, you die by Facebook, to paraphrase the old saying. Terrorist reliance on electronic media and forms of communication is also a weakness. Terrorists are not fools. They seek out and use the latest cryptographic devices and forms of communication and have taken to the offensive through computer hacking and electronic warfare. We cannot be complacent lest we lose a technological advantage. Some pundits like to say that the future of terrorism is electronic, and certainly they have entered the digital realm. However, we doubt the days of IEDs and bomb vests are over.

## Last Remarks

The world of terrorism and CT is messy and unwieldy. However, the relative complexity of this subject is no excuse for perpetuating easily and empirically refutable myths. We hope that you have gained some perspective on some simple realities that will help you navigate a complex and growing body of science (and fiction). If we have accomplished that, we have been successful.

## Note

1. Hudson et al. 2019.

# Bibliography

Aldoory, L., and M. Van Dyke. 2006. "The Roles of Perceived 'Shared' Involvement and Information Overload in Understanding How Audiences Make Meaning of News About Bioterrorism." *Journalism and Mass Communication Quarterly* 83, no. 2: 346–361.

Alesina, A., S. R. Ozler, and P. Swagel. 1996. "Political Instability and Economic Growth." *Journal of Economic Growth* 1: 189–211.

Ali, T. 2003. *The Clash of Fundamentalisms: Crusades, Jihads, and Modernity.* London: Verso.

Al-Obaidi, M., N. Abdullah, and S. Helfstein. 2009. "Deadly Vanguards—A Study of Al Qaeda's Violence Against Muslims." Combating Terrorism Center—West Point. December 1. ctc.usma.edu/deadly-vanguards-a-study -of-al-qaedas-violence-against-muslims.

Altemeyer, B. 1998. "The Other 'Authoritarian Personality.'" *Advances in Experimental Psychology* 30: 47–92.

American Psychological Association (APA). 2013. *Diagnostic and Statistical Manual of Mental Disorders.* 5th ed. Arlington, VA: APA.

Annan, K. 2002. "Statement to the International Conference on Financing for Development." March 21. www.un.org/ffd/pressrel/21a.htm.

Armstrong, K. 2000. *Islam.* New York: Modern Library.

Arndt, J., and M. Vess. 2008. "Tales from Existential Oceans: Terror Management Theory and How the Awareness of Our Mortality Affects All of Us." *Social and Personality Psychology Compass* 2: 909–928.

Asal, V., and K. Rethemeyer. 2008. "The Nature of the Beast: Organizational Structures and the Lethality of Terrorist Attacks." *Journal of Politics* 70, no. 2 (April): 437–449.

Atran, S. 2003. "Genesis of Suicide Terrorism." *Science* 299: 1534–1539.

————. 2014. "Jihad's Fatal Attraction." *Guardian*. September 4. www.theguardian .com/commentisfree/2014/sep/04/jihad-fatal-attraction-challenge-democrats -isis-barbarism.

Avalos, H. 2005. *Fighting Words: The Origins of Religious Violence*. Amherst, NY: Prometheus Books.

Avon, D., A. Khatchadourian, and J. Todd. 2012. *Hezbollah: A History of the "Party of God."* Cambridge, MA: Harvard University Press.

Azarva, J. 2009. "Is U.S. Detention Policy in Iraq Working?" *Middle East Quarterly* 16, no. 1 (winter): 5–14.

Baer, R. 2002. *See No Evil: The True Story of a Ground Soldier in the CIA's War Against Terrorism*. New York: Broadway Books.

Bandura, A. 1973. *Aggression: A Social Learning Analysis*. New York: Prentice Hall.

Bandura, A., D. Ross, and S. Ross. 1961. "Transmission of Aggression Through Imitation of Aggressive Models." *Journal of Abnormal and Social Psychology Review* 63: 575.

Barkun, M. 2014. *Religion and the Racist Right: The Origins of the Christian Identity Movement*. Chapel Hill: University of North Carolina Press.

Battle, S. 2010. "Lessons in Legitimacy: The LTTE End-Game of 2007–2009." Defense Technical Information Center. June. https://apps.dtic.mil/dtic/tr /fulltext/u2/a524509.pdf.

*BBC News*. 2014. "Public Appeal in Belgian Manhunt." *BBC News*. May 25. www.bbc.co.uk/news/world-europe-27567396.

Beaumont, C. 2008. "Mumbai Attacks: Twitter and Flickr Used to Break News." November 27. *Telegraph*. www.telegraph.co.uk/news/worldnews /asia/india/3530640/mumbai-attacks-twitter-and-flickr-used-to-break-news -bombay-india.html.

Becker, G. 1962. "Investment in Human Capital: A Theoretical Analysis." *Journal of Political Economy* 70, no. 5: 9–49.

————. 1968. "Crime and Punishment: An Economic Approach." In *The Economic Dimensions of Crime*, 13–68. London: Palgrave Macmillan.

————. 2005. "Terrorism and Poverty: Any Connection?" *Becker-Posner Blog*. May 29. http://becker-posner-blog.com/archives/2005/05.

Benmelech, E., and C. Berrebi. 2007. "Attack Assignments in Terror Organizations and the Productivity of Suicide Bombers." Working Paper 12910. National Bureau of Economic Research. February. www.nber.org/papers /w12910.

Bergen, P., and S. Pandey. 2005. "The Madrassa Myth." *New York Times*. June 14. www.nytimes.com/2005/06/14/opinion/the-madrassa-myth.html.

Berman, E. 2003. "Hamas, Taliban and the Jewish Underground: An Economist's View of Radical Religious Militias." Working Paper No. w10004. National Bureau of Economic Research. September 3. www.nber.org/papers /w10004.

Berman, E., and D. Laitin. 2008. "Religion, Terrorism, and Public Goods: Testing the Club Model." *Journal of Public Economics* 92: 1942–1967.

Berrebi, C. 2007. "Evidence About the Link Between Education, Poverty and Terrorism Among Palestinians." *Peace Economics, Peace Science and Public Policy* 13, no. 1: online: https://doi.org/10.2202/1554-8597.1101.

Bew, P. 2007. *The Making and Remaking of the Good Friday Agreement.* Dublin: Liffey Press.

Biçakei, S. 2007. "The Palestinian Parliamentary Legislative Elections 25 January 2006." *Journal of Southern Europe and the Balkans* 9, no. 1: 65–78.

Bier, J. 2014. "Kerry: 'Root Cause of Terrorism' Is Poverty." *Weekly Standard.* January 15. www.weeklystandard.com/kerry-root-cause-of-terrorism-is-poverty/article/774682.

Bishara, A. 1998. "Reflections and Realities of the Oslo Process." In *After Oslo: New Realities, Old Problems*, ed. G. Giacaman and D. Lonning. New York: Pluto Press.

Blankenship, B. 2018. "When Do States Take the Bait? State Capacity and the Provocation Logic of Terrorism." *Journal of Conflict Resolution* 62, no. 2: 381–409.

Bloom, M. 2004. "Palestinian Suicide Bombing: Public Support, Market Share, and Outbidding." *Political Science Quarterly* 119, no. 1: 61–88.

Boehmer, E. 2005. "Postcolonial Terrorist: The Example of Nelson Mandela." *Parallax* 11, no. 4: 46–55.

Bogacheva, P. 2016. *Theatre Security and Security Theatre.* New York: Columbia University. https://academiccommons.columbia.edu/doi/10.7916/D8MS3T3Z.

Bonner, D. 2000. "The United Kingdom's Response to Terrorism: The Impact of Decisions of European Judicial Institutions and of the Northern Ireland 'Peace Process.'" In *European Democracies Against Terrorism: Governmental Policies and Intergovernmental Cooperation*, ed. Fernando Reinares, 31–71. Aldershot, UK: Ashgate.

Bremer, P. 1992. "The West's Counter-terrorist Strategy." *Terrorism and Political Violence* 4, no. 4: 255–262.

Brown, R. 2003. "Spinning the War: Political Communications, Information Operations, and Public Diplomacy in the War on Terrorism." In *War and the Media*, ed. D. Kishan and D. Freedman. London: Sage Publishers.

Browne, J., and E. Dickson. 2010. "'We Don't Talk to Terrorists': On the Rhetoric and Practice of Secret Negotiations." *Journal of Conflict Resolution* 54, no. 3: 379–407.

Bruce Amstutz, J. 1994. *Afghanistan: The First Five Years of Soviet Occupation.* N.p.: Diane Publishing.

Brummette, J., L. Zoch, and L. Miller. 2013. "PETA: Media Reputation and Press Agency in the Context of Animal Rights Activism." Proceedings of the 16th International Public Relations Research Conference. Coral Gables, Florida, March 6–10, 124–139.

Bryant, E., M. Scott, C. Golden, and C. Tori. 1984. "Neurophysiological Deficits: Learning Disability and Violent Behavior." *Journal of Consulting and Clinical Psychology* 52: 323–324.

Buendo de Mesquita, E. 2005. "The Quality of Terror." *American Journal of Political Science* 49, no. 3 (July): 515–530.

Burke, B., A. Martens, and E. Faucher. 2010. "Two Decades of Terror Management Theory: A Meta Analysis of Mortality Salience Research." *Personality and Social Psychology Review* 14: 155–195.

Burnett, B. 2003. *The Attack on the USS Cole in Yemen on October 12, 2000.* New York: Rosen Publishing Group.

Bush, G. W. 2002. "Remarks at the International Conference on Financing for Development." United Nations. March 22. http://www.un.org/ffd/statements /usaE.htm.

Byman, D., and J. Shapiro. 2014. "Be Afraid. Be a Little Afraid: The Threat of Terrorism from Western Foreign Fighters in Syria and Iraq." Policy Paper No. 34. Brookings Institution. November. www.brookings.edu/wp-content /uploads/2016/06/Be-Afraid-web.pdf.

Cacioppo, J., and R. Petty. 1982. "The Need for Cognition." *Journal of Personality and Social Psychology* 42: 116–131.

Callimachi, R. 2018. "The ISIS Files." *New York Times*. April 4. www.nytimes .com/interactive/2018/04/04/world/middleeast/isis-documents-mosul-iraq .html.

Callimachi, R., and C. Porter. 2018. "Toronto Shooting Rekindles Familiar Debate. Terrorist? Mentally Ill? Both?" *New York Times*. July 25. www .nytimes.com/2018/07/25/world/americas/islamic-state-mental-health.html.

Campbell, D. 1958. "Common Fate, Similarity, and Other Indices of the Status of Aggregates of Persons as Social Entities." *Behavioral Science* 3: 14–25.

Canetti, D., and A. Pedahzur. 2002. "The Effects of Contextual and Psychological Variables on Extreme Rightwing Sentiments." *Social Behavior and Personality* 30: 17–34.

Chapman University. 2016. "What Do Americans Fear?" *Science News*. October 12. www.sciencedaily.com/releases/2016/10/161012160030.htm.

Chebab, Z. 2007. *Inside Hamas: The Untold Story of Militants, Martyrs, and Spies*. London: I. B. Tauris.

Chelin, R. 2018. "From the Islamic State of Algeria to the Economic Caliphate of the Sahel: The Transformation of Al Qaeda in the Islamic Maghreb." *Terrorism and Political Violence*. June 7. www.tandfonline.com/doi/full/10 .1080/09546553.2018.1454316.

Chesney, R. 2005. "Careful Thinking About Counterterrorism Policy." *Journal of National Security Law and Policy* 1: https://papers.ssrn.com/abstract =610585.

Ciment, J. 1997. *Algeria: The Fundamentalist Challenge*. New York: Facts on File, Inc.

Clutterbuck, R. 1992. "Negotiating with Terrorists." *Terrorism and Political Violence* 4, no. 4: 263–287.

Cohen, A. 2003. "Promoting Freedom and Democracy: Fighting the War of Ideas Against Islamic Terrorism." *Comparative Strategy* 22, no. 3: 207–221.

Cohen, T., M. Montoya, and C. Insko. 2006. "Group Morality and Intergroup Relations: Cross-cultural and Experimental Evidence." *Personality and Social Psychology Bulletin* 32, no. 11: 1559–1572.

Coll, S. 2004. *Ghost Wars: The Secret History of the CIA, Afghanistan, and Bin Laden, from the Soviet Invasion to September 10, 2001*. New York: Penguin Press.

———. 2018. *Directorate S: The C.I.A. and America's Secret Wars in Afghanistan and Pakistan*. London: Penguin.

Cook, D. 2008. *Contemporary Muslim Apocalyptic Literature*. Syracuse, NY: Syracuse University Press.

Cooper, H. 1977. "What Is a Terrorist: A Psychological Perspective." *Legal Medical Quarterly* 1: 16–32.

———. 1978. "Psychopath as Terrorist: A Psychological Perspective." *Legal Medical Quarterly* 2: 253–262.

Corner, E., and P. Gill. 2015. "A False Dichotomy? Mental Illness and Lone-Actor Terrorism." *Law and Human Behavior* 39: 23–34.

Cottman, M. 1994. *Images and Intervention: U.S. Policies in Latin America.* Pittsburgh, PA: University of Pittsburgh.

Crelinsten, R. 1998. "The Discourse and Practice of Counter-terrorism in Liberal Democracies." *Australian Journal of Politics and History* 44, no. 3: 389–413.

Crelinsten, R., and A. Schmid. 1992. "Western Response to Terrorism: A Twenty-Five Year Balance Sheet." *Terrorism and Political Violence* 4, no. 4: 307–340.

Crenshaw, M. 1981. "The Causes of Terrorism." *Comparative Politics* 13, no. 4: 379–399.

———. 1992. "How Terrorists Think: What Psychology Can Contribute to Understanding Terrorism." In *Terrorism: Roots, Impacts, Responses*, ed. L. Howard. New York: Praeger.

Davis, C. 1962. "Narodnaya Volya: Some Aspects of the Politics of a 19th Century Russian Political Movement." Ph.D. Dissertation.

Dechesne, M., T. Pyszczynski, J. Arndt, S. Ransom, K. Sheldon, van A. Knippensberg, and J. Janssen. 2003. "Literal and Symbolic Immortality: The Effect of Literal Immortality on Self-Esteem Striving in Response to Mortality Salience." *Journal of Personality and Social Psychology* 84: 722–737.

de la Corte Ibáñez, L. 2014. "Suicide Terrorism Explained: A Psychosocial Approach." In *Understanding Suicide Terrorism: Psychosocial Dynamics*, ed. Updesh Kumar and Manas K. Mandal, p. 36, Los Angeles, CA: Sage.

de Silva, K. 2012. *Sri Lanka and the Defeat of the LTTE.* London: Penguin.

Dickey, C. 2014. "French Jihadi Mehdi Nemmouche Is the Shape of Terror to Come." *Daily Beast.* September 9. www.thedailybeast.com/articles/2014/09/09/the-face-of-isis-terror-to-come.

Dodwell, B., D. Milton, and D. Rassler. 2016. *The Caliphate's Global Workforce: An Inside Look at the Islamic State's Foreign Fighter Paper Trail.* West Point, NY: US Military Academy, Combatting Terrorism Center.

Dollard, J., L. Dobb, N. Miller, E. Mowrer, and R. Sears. 1939. *Frustration and Aggression.* New Haven, CT: Yale University Press.

Dugas, M., J. Bélanger, M. Moyano, B. Schumpe, A. Kruglanski, M. Gelfand, and N. Nocin. 2016. "The Quest for Significance Motivates Self-Sacrifice." *Motivation Science* 2: 15–32.

Duyvesteyn, I. 2004. "How New Is the New Terrorism?" *Studies in Conflict and Terrorism* 27, no. 5: 439–454.

Easterly, W. 2017. "This Common Argument for U.S. Foreign Aid Is Actually Quite Xenophobic." *Washington Post.* March 31. www.washingtonpost.com/news/global-opinions/wp/2017/03/31/this-common-argument-for-u-s-foreign-aid-is-actually-quite-xenophobic.

Ekehammar, B., N. Akrami, M. Gylje, and I. Zakrisson. 2004. "What Matters Most to Prejudice: Big Five Personality, Dominance Orientation, or Right-Wing Authoritarianism." *European Journal of Personality* 18, no. 6: 463–482.

Enders, W., and T. Sandler. 2011. *The Political Economy of Terrorism*. Cambridge: Cambridge University Press.

Esposito, M. 2005. "The Al-Aqsa Intifada: Military Operations, Suicide Attacks, Assassinations, and Losses in the First Four Years." *Journal of Palestine Studies* 34, no. 2: 85–122.

Farwell, J. 2014. "The Media Strategy of ISIS." *Survival* 56, no. 6: 49–55.

Ferracuti, F. 1982. "A Sociopsychiatric Interpretation of Terrorism." *Annals of the American Academy of Political and Social Science* 463: 129–140.

Ferracuti, F., and F. Bruno. 1981. "Psychiatric Aspects of Terrorism in Italy." In *The Mad, the Bad, and the Different: Essays in Honor of Simon Dinitz*, ed. I. Barak-Glantz and C. Huff, 199–213. Lexington, MA: Lexington Books.

Festinger, L. 1954. "A Theory of Social Comparison Processes." *Human Relations* 7: 117–140.

*Fox News*. 2015. "State Department Spokeswoman Floats Jobs as Answer to ISIS." FoxNews.com. February 17. www.foxnews.com/politics/2015/02/17/state-department-spokeswoman-floats-jobs-as-answer-to-isis.html.

Franko, W., and N. W. Kelly. 2016. "Class Bias in Voter Turnout, Representation, and Income Inequality." *Perspectives on Politics* 14, no. 2: 351–368.

Freeman, T. J. 2004. *Winning the War of Ideas in the Global War on Terrorism*. Carlisle Barracks, PA: US Army War College.

Frey, B. 1971. "Why Do High Income People Participate More in Politics?" *Public Choice* 11: 101–105.

Friedland, N. 1992. "Becoming a Terrorist: Social and Individual Antecedents." In *Terrorism: Roots, Impacts, Responses*, ed. L. Howard. New York: Praeger.

Friedman, R., and J. Arndt. 2005. "Reexploring the Connection Between Terror Management Theory and Dissonance Theory." *Personality and Social Psychology Bulletin* 31: 1217–1225.

Friedman, T. 1983. "Truck Loaded with TNT Wrecks Headquarters of a Marine Unit." *New York Times*. October 23.

Gambeta, D., and S. Hertog. 2016. *Engineers of Jihad: The Curious Connection Between Violent Extremism and Education*. Princeton, NJ: Princeton University Press.

Garrison, A. 2004. "Defining Terrorism: Philosophy of the Bomb, Propaganda by Deed and Change Through Fear and Violence." *Criminal Justice Studies* 17, no. 3: 259–279.

Gates, B. 2017. "Bill Gates: Cutting Foreign Aid Makes America Less Safe." Time.com. March 17. http://time.com/4704550/bill-gates-cutting-foreign-aid-makes-america-less-safe.

Gause, F. 2014. "Beyond Sectarianism: The New Middle East Cold War." Brookings Doha Center Analysis Paper. Brookings. July 22. https://www.brookings.edu/research/beyond-sectarianism-the-new-middle-east-cold-war.

Gentzkow, M., and J. Shapiro. 2006. "Media Bias and Reputation." *Journal of Political Economy* 114, no. 2: 280–316.

George, A. 1991. *Western State Terrorism*. Cambridge, UK: Polity Press.

Ghaneabassiri, K. 2010. "Muslim Selves and the American Body Politic: Placing Major Nidal Malik Hassan's Case in a Broader Socio-historical Context." *International Journal of Applied Psychoanalytic Studies* 7, no. 3: 219–230.

Ghannam, J. 2011. *Social Media in the Arab World: Leading Up to the Uprisings of 2011*. Washington, DC: Center for International Media Assistance, National Endowment for Democracy.

Gill, P., and E. Corner. 2017. "There and Back Again: The Study of Mental Disorder and Terrorist Involvement." *American Psychologist* 72: 231–241.

Glueck, K. 2015. "Cruz Pledges Relentless Bombing to Destroy ISIL." *Politico.* December 12. www.politico.com/story/2015/12/cruz-isil-bombing-216454.

Goldman, L., and M. Hogg. 2016. "Going to Extremes for One's Own Group: The Role of Prototypicality and Group Acceptance." *Journal of Applied Social Psychology* 46: 544–553.

Greenberg, J., T. Pyszczynski, and S. Solomon. 1986. "The Causes and Consequences of a Need for Self-Esteem: A Terror Management Theory." In *Public and Private Self Help*, ed. R. Baumeister, 189–212. New York: Springer-Verlag.

Greenberg, J., S. Solomon, and T. Pyszczynski. 1997. "Terror Management Theory of Self-Esteem and Cultural Worldviews: Empirical Assessment and Conceptual Refinements." In *Advances in Experimental Social Psychology*, ed. M. Zanna, 29:61–139. New York: Academic Press.

Greenslade, R. 2015. "Why a 'War' on Terrorism Will Generate Yet More Terrorism." TheGuardian.com. November 30. www.theguardian.com/media/greenslade/2015/nov/30/why-a-war-on-terrorism-will-generate-yet-more-terrorism.

Greenwood, C. 2013. "The Twitter Terrorists: How Killers Boasted of Kenyan Mall Carnage with Live Commentary as They Murdered Dozens of People." *Daily Mail.* September 22. www.dailymail.co.uk/news/article-2429660/kenya-attack-how-killers-boasted-nairobi-westgate-shopping-mall-carnage-twitter.html.

Gregg, H. 2014. "Defining and Distinguishing Secular and Religious Terrorism." *Perspectives on Terrorism* 8, no. 2: 36–51.

Grieve, P., and M. Hogg. 1999. "Subjective Uncertainty and Intergroup Discrimination in the Minimal Group Situation." *Personality and Social Psychology Bulletin* 25: 926–940.

Gruenewald, J., S. Chermak, and J. Freilich. 2013. "Distinguishing 'Loner' Attacks from Other Domestic Extremist Violence." *Criminology Public Policy* 12: 65–91.

Gunning, J., and R. Jackson. 2011. "What's So Religious About Religious Terrorism?" *Critical Studies in Terrorism* 4, no. 3: 369–388.

Hacker, F. 1983. "Dialectic Interrelationships of Personal and Political Factors in Terrorism." In *Perspectives on Terrorism*, ed. L. Freedman and Y. Alexander, 19–31. Wilmington, DE: Scholarly Resources, Inc.

Hague, R., and M. Harrop. 2013. *Comparative Government and Politics: An Introduction*. New York: Macmillan Higher Education.

Haidt, J. 2013. *The Righteous Mind: Why Good People Are Divided by Politics and Religion*. New York: First Vintage Books.

Hallenbeck, R. A. 1991. *Military Force as an Instrument of U.S. Foreign Policy: Intervention in Lebanon, August 1982–February 1984*. Westport, CT: Greenwood Publishing Group.

Hamblen, J., and L. Sloan. 2016. "Research Findings on the Traumatic Stress Effects of Terrorism." National Center for PTSD. February 23. www.ptsd .va.gov/professional/trauma/disaster-terrorism/research-findings-traumatic -stress-terrorims.asp.

Hamieh, C., and R. Ginty. 2010. "A Very Political Reconstruction: Governance and Reconstruction in Lebanon After the 2006 War." *Disasters* 34 (Supplement 1): S103–S123.

Hamilton, D., and S. Sherman. 1996. "Perceiving Persons and Groups." *Psychological Review* 103: 336.

Hamzeh, A. 2004. *In the Path of Hizbullah.* Syracuse, NY: Syracuse University Press.

Harik, J. 2005. *Hezbollah: The Changing Face of Terrorism.* London: I. B. Tauris.

Hassan, N. 2001. "An Arsenal of Believers." *New Yorker* (November 19): 36–41.

Hayes, B., and I. McAllister. 1999. "Ethnonationalism, Public Opinion, and the Good Friday Agreement." In *After the Good Friday Agreement: Analyzing Political Change in Northern Ireland*, ed. J. Ruane and J. Todd, 30–48. Dublin: University College Dublin Press.

Hegghammer, T. 2006. "Terrorist Recruitment and Radicalization in Saudi Arabia." *Middle East Policy* 13, no. 4: 39–60.

———. 2013. "Should I Stay or Should I Go? Explaining Variation in Western Jihadists' Choice Between Domestic and Foreign Fighting." *American Political Science Review* 107, no. 1: 1–15.

Henry, P., J. Sidanius, S. Levin, and F. Pratto. 2005. "Social Dominance Orientation, Authoritarianism, and Support for Intergroup Violence Between the Middle East and America." *Political Psychology* 26: 569–584.

Herrmann, R., P. Tetlock, and P. Visser. 1999. "Mass Public Decisions to Go to War: A Cognitive-Interactionist Framework." *American Political Science Review* 93, no. 3: 553–573.

Heskin, K. 1984. "The Psychology of Terrorism." In *Terrorism in Ireland*, ed. Y. Alexander and A. O'Day. New York: St. Martin's.

Hills, A. 2002. "Responding to Catastrophic Terrorism." *Studies in Conflict and Terrorism* 25: 245–261.

Hiro, D. 1993. *Lebanon: Fire and Embers: A History of the Lebanese Civil War.* London, UK: Weidenfeld and Nicholson.

Hirschkorn, P., and P. Bergen. 2015. "Rare Photos Reveal Osama bin Laden's Afghan Hideout." CNN.com. March 18. www.cnn.com/2015/03/11/world /osama-bin-laden-hideout-photos/index.html.

Hoffman, B. 2006. *Inside Terrorism.* New York: Columbia University Press.

Hofstede, G. 1991. *Cultures and Organizations: Intercultural Cooperation and Its Importance for Survival: Software of the Mind.* London: McGraw-Hill.

Hogg, M. 2000. "Subjective Uncertainty Reduction Through Self-Categorization: A Motivational Theory of Social Identity Processes." *European Review of Social Psychology* 11: 223–255.

———. 2001. "A Social Identity Theory of Leadership." *Personality and Social Psychology Review* 5: 184–200.

———. 2005. "Uncertainty, Social Identity and Ideology." In *Advances in Group Processes*, ed. S. Thye and E. Lawler, 22:203–230. New York: Elsevier.

Hogg, M., and J. Adelman. 2013. "Uncertainty Identity Theory: Extreme Groups, Radical Behavior, and Authoritarian Leadership." *Journal of Social Issues* 69: 436–454.

Hogg, M., C. Meehan, and J. Farquharson. 2010. "The Solace of Radicalism: Self-Uncertainty and Group Identification in the Face of Threat." *Journal of Experimental Social Psychology* 46: 1061–1066.

Hogg, M., D. Sherman, J. Dierselhuis, A. Maitner, and G. Moffitt. 2007. "Uncertainty, Entitativity, and Group Identification." *Journal of Experimental Social Psychology* 43: 135–142.

Hohman, Z., A. Gaffney, and M. Hogg. 2017. "Who Am I if I Am Not Like My Group? Self-Uncertainty and Feeling Peripheral in a Group." *Journal of Experimental Social Psychology* 72: 125–132.

Hohman, Z., and M. Hogg. 2015. "Fearing the Uncertain: Self-Uncertainty Plays a Role in Mortality Salience." *Journal of Experimental Social Psychology* 57: 31–42.

Holtman, P. 2005. "The PLO Charters of 1964 and 1968 and the Hamas Charter of 1988." GRIN Verlag. https://www.grin.com/document/126346.

Horgan, J. 2003. "The Search for the Terrorist Personality." In *Terrorists, Victims, and Society: Psychological Perspectives on Terrorism and Its Consequences*, ed. A. Silke, 3–27. West Sussex, UK: John Wiley and Sons.

Howell, B. 2003. "Seven Weeks: The Making of the USA PATRIOT Act." *George Washington Law Review* 72: 1145.

Huddy, L., S. Feldman, C. Taber, and G. Lahav. 2005. "Threat, Anxiety, and Support for Antiterrorism Policies." *American Journal of Political Science* 49, no. 3: 593–608.

Huddy, L., N. Khatib, and T. Capelos. 2002. "The Polls-Trends: Reactions to the Terrorist Attacks of September 11, 2001." *Public Opinion Quarterly* 66, no. 3: 418–450.

Hudson, D., Z. Hohman, J. Alquist, B. Harris, E. Niedbala, and M. Prince. 2019. "The Impacts of Stress on Economic Decisions." *Journal of Behavioral Economics for Policy* 3, no. 1: 30–36.

Hudson, D., and J. Lusk. 2004. "Activists and Corporate Behavior in Food Processing and Retailing." *Journal of Agricultural and Resource Economics* 29, no. 1: 79–93.

Huntington, S. 1996. *The Clash of Civilizations*. New York: Simon and Schuster.

Iannaccone, L. R. 2006. "The Market for Martyrs." *Interdisciplinary Journal on Research on Religion* 2, no. 4 (January): 1–28.

Inglehart, R., and P. Norris. 2009. "The True Clash of Civilizations." *Foreign Policy*. November 4. https://foreignpolicy.com/2009/11/04/the-true-clash-of-civilizations.

Jackson, B. 2009. "Organizational Decisionmaking by Terrorist Groups." In *Social Science for Decision-Making: Putting the Pieces Together*, ed. P. Davis and K. Cragin, 209–255. Santa Monica, CA: Rand National Defense Research Institute.

Jäger, H., G. Schmidtchen, and L. Süllwold. 1981. *Analyzen zum Terrorismum 2: Lebenslaufanalysen*. Darmstadt, Germany: BeutscherVerlag.

Jenkins, B. 2010. *Would-Be Warriors: Incidents of Jihadist Terrorist Radicalization in the United States Since September 11, 2001*. Santa Monica, CA: Rand Corporation.

Jensen, R. 2013. *The Battle Against Anarchist Terrorism: An International History, 1878–1934*. New York: Cambridge University Press.

Johnson, E., and A. Tversky. 1983. *Affect, Generalization, and the Perception of Risk*. Springfield, VA: National Technical Information Service.

Jones, D., M. Smith, and M. Weeding. 2003. "Looking for the Pattern: Al Qaeda in Southeast Asia—The Geneology of a Terror Network." *Studies in Conflict and Terrorism* 26, no. 6: 443–457.

Jones, J. 2008. *Blood That Cries Out from the Earth: The Psychology of Religious Terrorism*. Oxford: Oxford University Press.

Juergensmeyer, M. 2000. *Terror in the Mind of God*. Berkeley: University of California Press.

———. 2013. "Religious Terrorism as Performance Violence." In *The Oxford Handbook of Religion and Violence*, ed. M. Jerryson, M. Juergensmeyer, and M. Kitts. Oxford: Oxford University Press.

Kahn, J., and T. Weiner. 2002. "World Leaders Rethinking Strategy on Aid to Poor." *New York Times*. March 18. www.newyorktimes.com.

Kallis, A. 2018. "The Radical Right and Islamaphobia." In *The Oxford Handbook of the Radical Right*, ed. J. Rydgren, 42–60. Oxford: Oxford University Press.

Kaplan, A. 1981. "The Psychodynamics of Terrorism." In *Behavioral and Quantitative Perspectives on Terrorism*, ed. Y. Alexander and J. Gleason, 35–50. New York: Pergamon.

Kean, T. 2011. *The 9/11 Commission Report: Final Report of the National Commission on Terrorist Attacks upon the United States*. Washington, DC: Government Printing Office.

Kellner, D. 2002. "September 11, Social Theory and Democratic Policies." *Theory, Culture and Society* 19, no. 4: 147–159.

Kelly, R., and R. Rieber. 1995. "Psychosocial Impacts of Terrorism and Organized Crime: The Counterfinality of the Practo-inert." *Journal of Social Distress and the Homeless* 4: 265–286.

Kepel, G. 2001. *Die Rache Gottes. Radikale Moslems, Christen und Juden auf dem Vormarsch*. Munchen: Piper.

Kerry, J. 2016, August 29. Press Conference. Bangladesh. http://bd.usembassy .gov/u-s-secretary-state-john-kerry-delivers-speech-u-s-bangladesh-relations.

Khan, R. 2011. "The Decline of Political Terrorism and the Rise of Religious Terrorism—Gene Expression." *Discover Magazine*. July 23. blogs .discovermagazine.com/gnxp/2011/07/the-decline-of-political-terrorism -the-rise-of-religious-terrorism.

Khatib, L., D. Matar, and A. Alshaer. 2014. *The Hizbullah Phenomenon: Politics and Communication*. Oxford: Oxford University Press.

Klausen, J. 2015. "Tweeting the Jihad: Social Media Networks of Western Foreign Fighters in Syria and Iraq." *Studies in Conflict and Terrorism* 38, no. 1: 1–22.

Klein, A. 2014. "Military Leaders Learned of Benghazi Deaths...Via Twitter?" *WorldNet Daily*. July 20. www.wnd.com/2014/07/military-learned-of -benghazi-deaths-via-twitter.

Koschade, S. 2006. "A Social Network Analysis of Jemaah Islamiyah: The Applications to Counterrorism and Intelligence." *Studies in Conflict and Terrorism* 29, no. 6: 559–575.

Kossowska, M., and M. Sekerdej. 2015. "Searching for Uncertainty: Religious Beliefs and Intolerance Toward Value-Violating Groups." *Personality and Individual Differences* 83: 72–76.

Kramer, M. 2005. "The Perils of Counterinsurgency: Russia's War in Chechnya." *International Security* 29, no. 3: 5–63.

Krueger, A., and D. Laitin. 2008. "Kto Kogo? A Cross-Country Study of the Origins and Targets of Terrorism." In *Terrorism, Economic Development, and Political Openness*, ed. Philip Keefer and Norman Loayza, 148–173. Cambridge: Cambridge University Press.

Krueger, A., and J. Malečková. 2003. "Education, Poverty and Terrorism: Is There a Causal Connection?" *Journal of Economic Perspectives* 17, no. 4: 119–144.

Krueger, R., S. South, W. Johnson, and W. Iacono. 2008. "The Heritability of Personality Is Not Always 50%: Gene-Environment Interactions and Correlation Between Personality and Parenting." *Journal of Personality* 76: 1485–1521.

Kruglanski, A., X. Chen, M. Dechesne, S. Fishman, and E. Orehek. 2009. "Fully Committed Suicide Bombers' Motivation and the Quest for Personal Significance." *Political Psychology* 30: 331–357.

Kruglanski, A., and S. Fishman. 2006. "The Psychology of Terrorism: 'Syndrome' Versus 'Tool' Perspectives." *Terrorism and Political Violence* 18: 193–215.

Kruglanski, A., M. Gelgand, J. Bélanger, A. Sheveland, M. Hetiarachchi, and R. Gunarama. 2014. "The Psychology of Radicalization and Deradicalization: How Significance Quest Impacts Violent Extremism." *Political Psychology* 35: 69–93.

Kruglanski, W., and E. Oreheek. 2011. "The Role of the Quest for Personal Significance in Motivating Terrorism." In *The Psychology of Social Conflict and Aggression*, ed. J. Forgas, A. Kruglanski, and K. Williams, 153–166. New York: Psychology Press.

Kurz, A. 2003. "'New Terrorism': New Challenges, Old Dilemmas." *Strategic Assessment* 6, no. 2 (September).

Lahav, G. 2004. *Immigration and Politics in the New Europe: Reinventing Borders*. Cambridge: Cambridge University Press.

Lambert, A., and A. Chasteen. 1997. "Perceptions of Disadvantage Versus Conventionality: Political Values and Attitudes Toward the Elderly Versus Blacks." *Personality and Social Psychology Bulletin* 23, no. 5: 469–481.

Lapidus, G. 2002. "Putin's War on Terrorism: Lessons from Chechnya." *Post-Soviet Affairs* 18, no. 1: 41–48.

Laqueur, W. 1999. *The New Terrorism: Fanaticism and the Arms of Mass Destruction*. New York: Oxford University Press.

Leavitt, M. 2015. *Hezbollah: The Global Footprint of Lebanon's Party of God*. Washington, DC: Georgetown University Press.

Lee, A. 2011. "Who Becomes a Terrorist? Poverty, Education, and the Origins of Political Violence." *World Politics* 63, no. 2 (April): 203–245.

Levine, S. 1999. "Youths in Terroristic Groups, Gangs, and Cults: The Allure, the Animus, and the Alienation." *Psychiatric Annals* 29: 342–349.

Lind, E., and K. van den Bos. 2002. "When Fairness Works: Toward a General Theory of Uncertainty Management." In *Research in Organizational Behavior*, ed. B. Staw and R. Kramer, 181–223. Greenwich, CT: JAI Press.

Lyons, J. 2014. "Brit Fanatics Returning from the Syria Conflict Pose the Biggest Terror Threat Since 9/11." *Daily Mirror*. February 25. www.mirror.co.uk/news/british-fighters-syria-terror-threat-3182881.

Mackey, R. 2014. "The Case for ISIS, Made in a British Accent." *New York Times*. June 20. www.nytimes.com/2014/06/21/world/middleeast/the-case-for-isis-made-in-a-british-accent.html.

Marine Corps Association. (n.d.). "DOD Commission Reports on Beirut Terrorist Attacks." Marine Corps Association. www.mca-marines.org/gazette/dod-commission-reports-beirut-terrorist-attack.

Marshall, T., and J. Danizewski. 2001. "Pakistan's Muslim Schools Offer a Dark View of the U.S." *Los Angeles Times*. September 9. A1.

Mastracci, D. 2015. "ISIL Members Decry Nepotistic Suicide Bomber Wait List, Demand Equal Opportunity to Blow Themselves Up." *National Post*. May 21. https://nationalpost.com/news/world/isil-members-decry-nepotistic-suicide-bomber-wait-list-demand-equal-opportunity-to-blow-themselves-up.

Matusitz, J., and M. Forrester. 2013. "PETA Making Social Noise: A Perspective on Shock Advertising." *Portuguese Journal of Social Science* 12, no. 1: 85–100.

McCann, S. 1997. "Threatening Times, 'Strong' Presidential Popular Vote Winners, and the Victory Margin." *Journal of Personality and Social Psychology* 73, no. 1: 160–170.

McElwee, S. 2014. "Why the Voting Gap Matters." Demos. October 23. http://www.demos.org/publication/why-voting-gap-matters.

McGregor, I. 2006. "Offensive Defensiveness: Toward an Integrative Neuroscience of Compensatory Zeal After Mortality Salience, Personal Uncertainty, and Other Poignant Self-Threats." *Psychology Inquiry* 17: 299–308.

McGregor, I., R. Haji, K. Nash, and R. Teper. 2008. "Religious Zeal and Uncertain Self." *Basic and Applied Social Psychology* 85: 183–188.

McGregor, I., and D. Marigold. 2003. "Defensive Zeal and Uncertain Self: What Makes You So Sure." *Journal of Personality and Social Psychology* 85: 838–852.

McMichael, S. 2002. "The Soviet-Afghan War." In *The Military History of the Soviet Union*, ed. R. Higham and F. Kagan, 259–274. New York: Palgrave Macmillan.

Merari, A. 1998. "The Readiness to Kill and Die: Suicidal Terrorism in the Middle East." In *Origins of Terrorism: Psychologies, Ideologies, Theologies, States of Mind*, ed. W. Reich, 192–207. Washington, DC: Woodrow Wilson Center Press.

———. 2010. *Driven to Death: Psychological and Social Aspects of Suicide Terrorism*. Oxford: Oxford University Press.

Merari, A., I. Diamant, A. Bibi, Y. Broshi, and G. Zakin. 2009. "Personality Characteristics of 'Self-Martyrs'/'Suicide Bombers' and Organizers of Suicide Attacks." *Terrorism and Political Violence* 22: 87–101.

Milgram, P., and J. Roberts. 1992. *Economics, Organisations, and Management*. Englewood Cliffs, NJ: Prentice Hall.

Milton, D. 2016. "Communication Breakdown: Unraveling the Islamic State's Media Efforts." Combating Terrorism Center—West Point. https://ctc.usma.edu/communication-breakdown-unraveling-the-islamic-states-media-efforts.

Mishal, S., and M. Rosenthal. 2005. "Al Qaeda as a Dune Organization: Towards a Typology of Islamic Terrorist Organizations." *Studies in Conflict and Terrorism* 28: 275–293.

Mishal, S., and A. Sela. 2006. *The Palestinian Hamas: Vision, Violence, and Coexistence.* New York: Columbia University Press.

Mockaitis, T. 2008. *The "New" Terrorism: Myths and Reality.* Palo Alto, CA: Stanford University Press.

Murray, C. 2013. *Coming Apart: The State of White America, 1960–2010.* New York: Crown Publishing Group.

Mustapha, J. 2013. "The Mujahideen in Bosnia: The Foreign Fighter as Cosmopolitan Citizen and/or Terrorist." *Citizenship Studies* 17, no. 6–7: 742–755.

Nacos, B. 2016. *Mass-Mediated Terrorism: Mainstream and Digital Media in Terrorism and Counterterrorism.* 3rd ed. Lanham, MD: Rowman & Littlefield.

Neumann, P. 2007. "Negotiating with Terrorists." In *Democratic Responses to Terrorism,* 103–112. New York: Routledge.

Niedbala, E., and Z. Hohman. 2019. "Retaliation Against the Outgroup: The Role of Self-Uncertainty." *Group Processes and Intergroup Relations* 22, no. 5 (August): 708–723.

Niedbala, E., Z. Hohman, B. Harris, and A. Abide. 2018. "Taking One for the Team: Physiological Trajectories of Painful Intergroup Retaliation." *Physiology and Behavior* 194: 277–284.

Norris, P., and R. Inglehart. 2002. "Islamic Culture and Democracy: Testing the 'Clash of Civilizations' Thesis." *Comparative Sociology* 1, no. 3: 235–263.

Nussio, E. 2017. "The Role of Sensation Seeking in Violent Armed Group Participation." *Terrorism and Political Violence.* DOI: 10.1080/09546553.2017 .1342633.

Pahran, G., A. Pedahzur, and A. Perliger. 2005. *Countering Terrorism in Jerusalem: 1967–2002.* Hebrew ed. Jerusalem: Jerusalem Institute.

Panah, M. 2007. *The Islamic Republic and the World: Global Dimensions of the Iranian Revolution.* London: Pluto Press.

Pape, R. 2003. "The Strategic Logic of Suicide Terrorism." *American Political Science Review* 93, no. 3. https://www.cambridge.org/core/journals/american -political-science-review/article/strategic-logic-of-suicide-terrorism/A6F51 C77E3DE644EBD20ADE176973547.

———. 2005. *Dying to Win: The Strategic Logic of Suicide Terrorism.* New York: Random House.

Pearce, K. 1977. "Police Negotiations." *Canadian Psychiatric Association Journal* 22: 1–4.

Pearlman, W. 2011. "The Oslo Peace Process, 1993–2000." In *Violence, Nonviolence, and the Palestinian National Movement,* 124–149. Cambridge: Cambridge University Press.

Pedahzur, A. 2005. *Suicide Terrorism.* Cambridge, UK: Polity.

Pedahzur, A., and A. Perliger. 2006. "The Changing Nature of Suicide Attacks: A Social Network Perspective." *Social Forces: A Scientific Medium of Social Study and Interpretation* 84, no. 4: 1987–2008.

———. 2010. "The Consequences of Counterterrorist Policies in Isreal." In *The Consequences of Counterterrorism,* ed. M. Crenshaw, 335–366. New York: Russell Sage Foundation.

———. 2011. *Jewish Terrorism in Israel*. New York: Columbia University Press.

Pedahzur, A., A. Perliger, and L. Weinburg. 2003. "Altruism and Fatalism: The Characteristics of Palestinian Suicide Terrorists." *Deviant Behavior* 24: 405–423.

Pedahzur, A., and M. Ranstorp. 2001. "A Tertiary Model for Countering Terrorism in Liberal Democracies: The Case of Israel." *Terrorism and Political Violence* 13, no. 2: 1–26.

Peres, S. 2015. "Shimon Peres, Tony Blair Say Solving Poverty Will End Cause of Terror." *YES*. September 11. https://yes-ukraine.org/en/news/shimon-peres-zaklikaye-borotisya-z-prichinoyu-teroru-bidnistyu.

Perez-Peña, R. 2017. "A Look at Dylann Roof's Rampage and Its Aftermath." *New York Times*. January 10. https://www.nytimes.com/2017/01/10/us/dylann-roof-trial-sentencing-verdict.html.

Perliger, A. 2012a. *Challengers from the Sidelines: Understanding America's Violent Far Right*. West Point, NY: US Military Academy, Combating Terrorism Center.

———. 2012b. "How Democracies Respond to Terrorism: Regime Characteristics, Symbolic Power, and Counterterrorism." *Security Studies* 21, no. 3: 490–528.

———. 2017. "The Role of Civil Wars and Elections in Inducing Political Assassinations." *Studies in Conflict and Terrorism* 40, no. 8: 684–700.

Perliger, A., B. Hasisi, and A. Pedahzur. 2009. "Policing Terrorism in Israel." *Criminal Justice and Behavior* 36, no. 12: 1279–1304.

Perliger, A., and D. Milton. 2016. *From Cradle to Grave: The Life Cycle of Foreign Fighters in Iraq and Syria*. West Point, NY: US Military Academy, Combating Terrorism Center.

———. 2018. "Fighting Together? Understanding Bilateral Cooperation in the Realm of Counterterrorism." *Dynamics of Asymmetric Conflict* 11, no. 3: 199–220.

Perliger, A., and A. Pedahzur. 2014. "Counter Cultures, Group Dynamics, and Religious Terrorism." *Political Studies* 64, no. 2: 297–314.

Perliger, A., A. Pedahzur, and Y. Zalmanovitch. 2005. "The Defensive Dimension of the Battle Against Terrorism: An Analysis of Management of Terror Incidents in Jerusalem." *Journal of Contingencies and Crisis Management* 13, no. 2: 79–91.

Perry, R. 2003. "Emergency Operations Centers in an Era of Terrorism: Policy and Management Functions." *Journal of Contingencies and Crisis Management* 11, no. 4: 151–159.

Person, E. 2011. "U.S. Marine Barracks Bombing, Beirut." In *The SAGE Encyclopedia of Terrorism*, ed. G. Martin. London, UK: Sage Publishers.

Philpott, D. 2013. "Religion and Violence from a Political Perspective." In *The Oxford Handbook of Religion and Violence*, ed. M. Juergensmeyer, M. Kitts, and M. Jerryson. Oxford: Oxford University Press.

Post, J. 1998. "Terrorist Psycho-Logic: Terrorist Behavior as a Product of Psychological Forces." In *Origins of Terrorism: Psychologies, Ideologies, Theologies, States of Mind*, ed. W. Reich, 25–40. Washington, DC: Woodrow Wilson Center Press.

———. 2004. *Leaders and Their Followers in a Dangerous World: The Psychology of Political Behavior*. Ithaca, NY: Cornell University Press.

Post, J., E. Sprinzak, and L. Denny. 2003. "The Terrorists in Their Own Words: Interviews with Thirty-Five Incarcerated Middle Eastern Terrorists." *Terrorism and Political Violence* 15: 171–184.

Post, R., D. Hudson, D. Mitchell, P. Bell, A. Perliger, and R. Williams. 2016. "Rethinking the Water-Food-Climate Nexus and Conflict: An Opportunity Cost Approach." *Applied Economics Perspectives and Policy* 38, no. 4: 563–577.

Post, T. H. 2010. "PETA Protests with 'Human Meat' Demonstration in Times Square." *Huffington Post*. July 28. www.huffingtonpost.com/2010/07/28/peta-protests-with-human_n_662087.html.

Poteat, V., and E. Mereish. 2012. "Ideology, Prejudice, and Attitudes Toward Sexual Minority Social Policies and Organizations." *Political Psychology* 33, no. 2: 211–224.

Pratto, F., J. Sidanius, L. Stallworth, and F. Bertram. 1994. "Social Dominance Orientation: A Personality Variable Predicting Social and Political Attitudes." *Journal of Personality and Social Psychology* 67, no. 4: 741–763.

Pyszczynski, T., A. Abdollahi, J. Greenberg, and S. Solomon. 2006. "Crusades and Jihads: An Existential Psychological Perspective on the Psychology of Terrorism and Political Extremism." In *Tangled Roots: Social and Psychological Factors in the Genesis of Terrorism*, ed. J. Victoroff, 85–97. Amsterdam: IOS Press.

Pyszczynski, T., J. Greenberg, S. Solomon, J. Arndt, and J. Schimel. 2004. "Why Do People Need Self-Esteem? A Theoretical and Empirical Review." *Psychological Bulletin* 130: 435.

Pyszczynski, T., Z. Rothschild, and A. Abdollahi. 2008. "Terrorism, Violence, and Hope for Peace: A Terror Management Perspective." *Current Directions in Psychological Science* 17: 318–322.

Quarles, C. 2004. *Christian Identity: The Aryan American Bloodline Religion.* Jefferson, NC: McFarland.

Qureshi, E., and M. Sells. 2003. *The New Crusades: Constructing the Muslim Enemy.* New York: Columbia University Press.

Radu, M. 2004. *The Futile Search for "Root Causes" of Terrorism.* Philadelphia: Foreign Policy Research Institute.

Rapoport, D. 1983. "Fear and Trembling: Terrorism in Three Religious Traditions." *American Political Science Review* 78, no. 3: 658–677.

———. 2013. "The Four Waves of Modern Terrorism." In *Terrorism Studies: A Reader*, ed. J. Horgan and K. Braddock, 63–82. New York: Taylor and Francis.

Rasch, W. 1979. "Psychological Dimensions of Political Terrorism in the Federal Republic of Germany." *International Journal of Law and Psychiatry* 2: 79–85.

Raufer, X. 2003. "Al Qaeda: A Different Diagnosis." *Studies in Conflict and Terrorism* 26: 391–398.

Raworth, S. (n.d.). "D-day 75: How Was the Biggest Ever Seaborne Invasion Launched?" *BBC Teach.* https://www.bbc.co.uk/teach/d-day-how-was-the-biggest-ever-seaborne-invasion-launched/zrrs7nb.

Reich, W. 1998. "Understanding Terrorist Behavior: The Limits and Opportunities of Psychological Inquiry." In *Origins of Terrorism: Psychologies, Ideologies, Theologies, States of Mind*, ed. W. Reich, 261–279. Washington, DC: Woodrow Wilson Center Press.

Reina, E. 2016. "Asesinado a Balazos el Alcalde de Jilotzingo, México." *El Pais.* April 22. https://elpais.com/internacional/2016/04/22/mexico/1461346190 _351973.html.

Renard, J. 2012. *Fighting Words: Religion, Violence, and the Interpretation of Sacred Texts.* Berkeley: University of California Press.

Ressler, S. 2006. "Social Network Analysis as an Approach to Combat Terrorism: Past, Present, and Future Research." *Homeland Security Affairs* 2, no. 2.

Robbins, J. 2017. "Does Military Intervention Increase the Terror Threat?" BBC.com. May 26. www.bbc.com/news/uk-40061551.

Roberts, C. 2003. *Race over Grace: The Racist Religion of the Christian Identity Movement.* N.p.: iUniverse Publishers.

Robinson, G. 2010. "Al-Aqsa Intifada 10 Years Later." *Foreign Policy.* October 18. http://mideasafrica.foreignpolicy.com/posts/2010/10/18/the_al_aqsa _10_years_later.

Rohner, D., and B. Frey. 2007. "Blood and Ink! The Common-Interest-Game Between Terrorists and the Media." *Public Choice* 133: 129–145.

Russell, C., and B. Miller. 1983. "Profile of a Terrorist." In *Perspectives in Terrorism*, ed. L. Z. Feedman and Y. Alexander, 45–60. Wilmington, DE: Scholarly Resources Inc.

Sageman, M. 2004. *Understanding Terror Networks.* Philadelphia: University of Pennsylvania Press.

Satterfield, M. 1998. "Cognitive-Affective States Predict Military and Political Aggression and Risk Taking: A Content Analysis of Churchill, Hitler, Roosevelt, and Stalin." *Journal of Conflict Resolution* 42: 667–690.

Saud, L. 2016. *The Legacy of 9/11: A Divisive, Self-Fulfilling, Global Prophecy. Alarby: The New Arab.* September 13. www.alarby.co.uk/english /comment/2016/9/13/the-legacy-of-9-11-a-divisive-self-fulfilling-prophecy.

Schmid, A. 1988. "Force of Conciliation? An Overview of Some Problems Associated with Current Anti-terrorist Response Strategies." *Violence, Aggression and Terrorism* 2, no. 2: 149–178.

———. 1992. "Terrorism and Democracy." *Terrorism and Political Violence* 4, no. 4: 14–25.

Schmid, A., and A. Longman. 2005. *Political Terrorism: A New Guide to Actors, Authors, Concepts, Data Bases, Theories and Literature.* New Brunswick, NJ: Transactions Publishers.

Schulze, K. 2001. "Camp David and the Al-Aqsa Intifada: An Assessment of the State of the Israeli-Palestinian Peace Process, July–December 2000." *Studies in Conflict and Terrorism* 24, no. 3: 215–233.

Schumpe, B., J. Belanger, M. Moyano, and C. Nisa. 2018. "The Role of Sensation Seeking in Political Violence: An Extension of the Significance Quest Theory." *Journal of Personality and Social Psychology.* November 1. http://dx.doi.org/10.1037/pspp0000223.

Sederberg, P. 1995. "Conciliation as a Counter-terrorism Strategy." *Journal of Peace Research* 32, no. 3: 295–312.

Sekerdej, M., M. Kossowska, and A. Czernatowicz-Kukeczka. 2018. "Uncertainty and Prejudice: The Role of Religiosity in Shaping Attitudes." *European Journal of Social Psychology* 48: O91–O102.

Selden, M., and A. So, ed. 2004. *War and State Terrorism: The United States, Japan, and the Asia-Pacific in the Long Twentieth Century*. Lanham, MD: Rowman & Littlefield Publishers.

Shane, S., and B. Hubbard. 2014. "ISIS Displaying a Deft Command of Varied Media." *New York Times*. August 30. www.nytimes.com/2014/08/31 /world/middleeast/isis-displaying-a-deft-command-of-caried-media.html.

Shapiro, J. 2013. *The Terrorist's Dilemma: Managing Violent Covert Organizations*. Princeton, NJ: Princeton University Press.

Shaver, A. 2015. "You're More Likely to Be Fatally Crushed by Furniture Than Killed by a Terrorist." *Washington Post*. November 23. www.washingtonpost .com/news/monkey-cage/wp/2015/11/23/youre-more-likely-to-be-fatally -crushed-by-furniture-than-killed-by-a-terrorist.

Sherman, E. 2008. "E-Conglomerates: Smart Strategy or Future Problem?" CBSNews.com. August 5. www.cbsnews.com/news/e-conglomerates-smart -strategy-or-future-problem.

Silke, A. 1998. "Cheshire-Cat Logic: The Recurring Theme of Terrorist Abnormality in Psychological Research." *Psychology, Law, and Crime* 4: 51–69.

Singer, P. 2012. "The Evolution of Improvised Explosive Devices (IEDs)." Brookings. February 7. www.brookings.edu/articles/the-evolution-of-improvised -explosive-devices-ieds.

Singman, B. 2016. "House Report: U.S. Facing Biggest Islamic Terror Threat Since 9/11." *Fox News*. December 6. www.foxnews.com/us/2016/12/06 /house-report-us-facing-biggest-islamic-terror-threat-since-911.html.

Sly, L. 2014. "Al-Qaeda Disavows Any Ties with Radical Islamist ISIS Group in Syria, Iraq." WashingtonPost.com. February 3. www.washingtonpost.com /world/middle_east/al-qaeda-disavows-any-ties-with-radical-islamist-isis -group-in-syria-iraq/2014/02/03/2c9afc3a-8cef-11e3-98ab-fe5228217bd1 _story.html.

Sprinzak, E. 1989. "The Emergence of the Israeli Radical Right." *Comparative Politics* 21, no. 2: 171.

———. 1991. *The Ascendence of Isreal's Radical Right*. Oxford: Oxford University Press.

Stephan, W., and C. Renfro. 2002. "The Role of Threat in Intergroup Relations." In *From Prejudice to Intergroup Emotions: Differentiated Reactions to Social Groups*, ed. D. Mackie and E. Smith, 191–207. New York: Psychology Press.

Stern, J. 2009. *Terror in the Name of God: Why Religious Militants Kill*. New York: Harper Collins.

Stewart, M., B. Ellingwood, and J. Mueller. 2011. "Homeland Security: A Case Study in Risk Aversion for Public Decision-Making." *International Journal of Risk Management* 15, no. 5/6: 367–386.

Strentz, T. 1988. "A Terrorist Psychosocial Profile: Past and Present." *FBI Law Enforcement Bulletin* 57: 13–19.

Suedfeld, P., P. Tetlock, and S. Streudfert. 1992. "Conceptual/Integrative Complexity." In *Motivation and Personality: Handbook of Thematic Content Analysis*, ed. C. Smith, J. Atkinson, D. McClelland, and J. Veroff, 393–400. New York: Cambridge University Press.

Tan, A., T. Huat, and K. Ramakrishna. 2002. *The New Terrorism: Anatomy, Trends, and Counter-strategies*. Singapore: Marshall Cavendish Academic.

Taylor, M., and E. Quayle. 1994. *Terrorist Lives*. London: Brassey's.

Thompson, P. 2004. *The Terror Timeline: Year by Year, Day by Day, Minute by Minute: A Comprehensive Chronicle of the Road to 9/11—and America's Response*. New York: Harper Collins.

Thompson, R. 2011. "Radicalization and the Use of Social Media." *Journal of Strategic Security* 4, no. 4: 167–190.

Thomsen, L., E. Green, and J. Sidanius. 2008. "We Will Hunt Them Down: How Social Dominance Orientation and Right-Wing Authoritarianism Fuel Ethnic Persecution of Immigrants in Fundamentally Different Ways." *Journal of Experimental Social Psychology* 44: 1455–1464.

Thrall, A., and E. Groepner. 2017. "Step Back: Lessons for U.S. Foreign Policy from the Failed War on Terror." Policy Analysis No. 814. Cato Institute. June 26. https://papers.ssrn.com/abstract=3040878.

Toft, M. 2007. "Getting Religion? The Puzzling Case of Islam and Civil War." *International Security* 31, no. 4: 97–131.

Toros, H. 2008. "'We Don't Negotiate with Terrorists!' Legitimacy and Complexity in Terrorist Conflicts." *Security Dialogue* 39, no. 4: 407–426.

Towers, J. 2002. "The French in Algeria, 1954–1962: Military Success Failure of Grand Strategy." Defense Technical Information Center. April 9. https://doi.org/10.21236/ADA404412.

Turner, J., M. Hogg, P. Oakes, S. Reicher, and M. Wetherell. 1987. *Rediscovering the Social Group: A Self-Categorization Theory*. Oxford, UK: Blackwell.

United Nations Security Council (UNSC). 2015. "Analysis and Recommendations with Regard to the Global Threat from Foreign Terrorist Fighters." UNSC. www.un.org/en/sc/ctc/docs/2015/N1508457_EN.pdf.

United States Agency for International Development (USAID). 2019. "Foreign Aid Explorer." USAID. May. https://explorer.usaid.gov/aid-trends.html.

van den Bos, K., P. Poortvliet, M. Maas, J. Miedeman, and van den E. Ham. 2005. "An Enquiry Concerning the Principles of Cultural Norms and Values: The Impact of Uncertainty and Mortality Salience on Reactions to Violations and Bolstering of Cultural Worldviews." *Journal of Experimental Social Psychology* 41: 91–113.

Victoroff, J. 2005. "The Mind of the Terrorist: A Review and Critique of Psychological Approaches." *Journal of Conflict Resolution* 49: 3–42.

Viscusi, K. 1990. "Do Smokers Underestimate Risks?" *Journal of Political Economy*, 1253–1269.

Vlahos, M. (n.d.). "About Beheading: There Is More to ISIS Decapitations Than Mere Publicity." *Huffington Post*. www.huffingtonpost.com/michael -vlahos/about-beheading-there-is-_b_5953098.html.

von Borcke, A. 1982. "Violence and Terror in Russian Revolutionary Populism: The Narodnay Volva, 1879–1883." In *Social Protest, Violence and Terror in Nineteenth- and Twentieth-Century Europe*, ed. W. Mommsen and G. Hirschfeld, 48–62. London: Palgrave Macmillan.

Watanabe, T. 2002. "Clinton Says U.S. Must Give More to End Terrorism." *Los Angeles Times*. January 15. http://articles.latimes.com/2002/jan/15/local /me-22657.

Watts, C. 2008. "Foreign Fighters: How Are They Being Recruited? Two Imperfect Recruitment Models." HomelandSecurity.org. www.homelandsecurity .org/hsireports/Internet_Radicalization.pdf.

Webster, D., and A. Kruglanski. 1994. "Individual Differences in Need for Cognitive Closure." *Journal of Personality and Social Psychology* 67: 1049–1062.

Weimann, G., and C. Winn. 1994. *Theater of Terror: Mass Media and International Terrorism*. White Plains, NY: Longman Publishing Group.

Weinberg, L., A. Pedahzur, and S. Hirsch. Hoefler. 2004. "The Challenges of Conceptualizing Terrorism." *Terrorism and Political Violence* 16, no. 4: 777–794.

Wessinger, C. 2009. "Deaths in the Fire at the Branch Davidians' Mount Caramel: Who Bears Responsibility?" *Nova Religio* 13, no. 2: 25–60.

Wharton School of Business. 2013. "Will Microsoft's Reorganization Pay Off?" Knowledge@Wharton. July 7. http://knowledge.wharton.upenn.edu/article/will-microsofts-reorganization-pay-off.

Wheeler, N. 2017. "Dying for 'Enduring Freedom': Accepting Responsibility for Civilian Casualties in the War Against Terrorism." In *War on Terrorism*, ed. A. O'Day, 107–127. 1st ed. New York: Routledge.

Whitehouse, H. 2013. "Religion, Cohesion, and Hostility." In *Religion, Intolerance, and Conflict*, ed. S. Clarke, R. Powell, and J. Savulescu, 36–47. Oxford: Oxford University Press.

Wiktorowicz, Q. 2006. "Anatomy of the Salafi Movement." *Studies in Conflict and Terrorism* 29, no. 3: 207–239.

Wilgoren, J. 2001. "After the Attacks: The Hijackers; A Terrorist Profile Emerges That Confounds the Experts." *New York Times*. September 15. A2.

Wilkinson, P. 1977. *Terrorism and the Liberal State*. New York: Macmillan Press.

Williamson, O. 1979. "Transaction-Cost Economics: The Governance of Contractual Relations." *Journal of Law and Economics* 22: 233–261.

Worrall, J., S. Mabon, and G. Clubb. 2015. *Hezbollah: From Islamic Resistance to Government*. Santa Barbara, CA: ABC-CLIO.

Worth, K. 2016. "Lone Wolf Attacks Are Becoming More Common—and More Deadly." PBS.org. July 14. www.pbs.org/wgbh/frontline/article/lone-wolf-attacks-are-becoming-more-common-and-more-deadly.

Wright, L. 2006. *The Looming Tower: Al-Qaeda and the Road to 9/11*. New York: Knopf.

Yang, Z., K. Coble, and D. Hudson. 2009. "The Role of Individual Personality Type in Subjective Risk Elicitation Outcomes." *Journal of Risk Research* 12, no. 2: 209–222.

Zuckerman, M. 1979. *Sensation Seeking: Beyond the Optimal Level of Arousal*. Hillsdale, NJ: Erlbaum.

# Index

# About the Book

Opinion surveys show that what the public assumes it knows about terrorism is at best a badly distorted view. Recalling the "Flat Earth" phenomenon, early misconceptions have become solidified, despite new evidence refuting them.

The authors of *The Irrational Terrorist* discredit these popular myths and misconceptions, providing an accessible overview of the realities of terrorism and liberally illustrating their analysis with case studies. Ranging from the religious and economic backgrounds of individual terrorists to the nature and outreach of terrorist organizations, they offer fact-based, cutting-edge explanations of the motivations and behavior of terrorist groups.

**Darren Hudson** is professor and Larry Combest Endowed Chair for Agricultural Competitiveness at Texas Tech University. **Arie Perliger** is professor and director of security studies at the University of Massachusetts Lowell. **Riley Post**, a Special Forces officer in the US Army, is currently assigned to the US Military Academy. **Zachary Hohman** is associate professor of experimental social psychology at Texas Tech University.